MODERN U.S. NAVY
DESTROYERS

S.F. Tomajczyk

MBI Publishing Company

Dedication

Dedicated to the crew of the USS Cole (DDG-67) and the entire Navy family.

First published in 2001 by MBI Publishing Company, 729 Prospect Avenue, PO Box 1, Osceola, WI 54020-0001 USA

The information in this book is true and complete to the best of our knowledge. All recommendations are made without any guarantee on the part of the author or Publisher, who also disclaim any liability incurred in connection with the use of this data or specific details.

We recognize that some words, model names and designations, for example, mentioned herein are the property of the trademark holder. We use them for identification purposes only. This is not an official publication.

MBI Publishing Company books are also available at discounts in bulk quantity for industrial or sales-promotional use. For details write to Special Sales Manager at Motorbooks International Wholesalers & Distributors, 729 Prospect Avenue, PO Box 1, Osceola, WI 54020-0001 USA.

Library of Congress Cataloging-in-Publication Data Available

ISBN 0-7603-0869-1

On the front cover: Aerial bow view of the USS McFaul (DDG-74) during sea trials. *Litton Ingalls Shipbuilding*

On the frontispiece: A close look at the Radar System Controller (RSC) console in the *Fitzgerald's* combat information center. The RSC oversees the four SPY-1D antennas mounted on the four corners of the ship's superstructure. *S. F. Tomajczyk*

On the title page: A beautiful perspective of the USS *Spruance* (DD-963), the lead ship of the destroyer class. *Litton Ingalls Shipbuilding*

On the back cover: Welcome to the dark world of the USS *Fitzgerald's* Combat Information Center. The CIC is where the data collected from the ships sensors is analyzed. *S.F. Tomajczyk*

Edited by Amy Glaser
Design and layout by Dan Perry

Printed in China

CONTENTS

ACKNOWLEDGMENTS

The comment "You have to serve on a destroyer if you really want to know what the Navy is about" is often made by Navy veterans, especially those who went to sea during World War II or the Cold War. That is because they were at the heart of anything and everything that happened at sea. While I am much too old to enlist in the Navy, I did the next best thing: I visited three front-line destroyers in service with the Atlantic and Pacific fleets to gain a better understanding of how these warships are used to project power and preserve peace around the world.

The writing of any book relies on trust and collaboration, and *Modern U.S. Navy Destroyers* is no different. I owe a great deal of thanks to many people, including the sailors who escorted me around their destroyers. Most notably, I extend my heartfelt appreciation to the following individuals who went above and beyond the call of duty to assist me in making this book a reality:

Commander Matthew S. Brown, force public affairs officer, Naval Surface Force, Pacific Fleet; Lieutenant Commander Dawn E. Cutler, deputy public affairs officer, Naval Surface Force, Pacific Fleet; Lieutenant Junior Grade (jg) James Hamilton, special projects officer, Naval Surface Force, Pacific Fleet; Lieutenant Robert Mehal, public affairs officer, Chief of Information Office (CHINFO); Ensign Susan Henson, public affairs officer, CHINFO; Christopher J. Madden, director, Navy News Still Photography Library, CHINFO; Lieutenant Rick Naystatt, deputy director, Navy News Still Photography Library, CHINFO; JOC David Rourk, media action officer, Commander in Chief, U.S. Atlantic Fleet (CINCLANTFLT); Barry Higginbotham, deputy for media, CINCLANTFLT; Captain William D. Crowder, commander, Destroyer Squadron 24; Commander Roger Coldiron, Commanding Officer (CO), USS *Stump* (DD-978); Commander James S.

Grant, CO, USS *Fitzgerald* (DDG-62); Lieutenant Commander Jesse Wilson, Executive Officer (XO), USS *Fitzgerald* (DDG-62); Ensign Marcus Kaiser, public affairs, USS *Fitzgerald* (DDG-62); Leading Chief Petty Officer Kent Haywood, USS *Fitzgerald* (DDG-62); Lieutenant (jg) Tom Post, USS *Fitzgerald* (DDG-62); Commander Donald Babcock, CO, USS *Oldendorf* (DD-972); and Lieutenant Trish Snyder, Nav/Admin Officer, USS *Oldendorf* (DD-972).

For their contribution of background information, technical specifications, and photographs, I also want to acknowledge Bath Iron Works Corporation (J. F. "Rusty" Robertson), United Defense LP (E. Jeffrey Van Keuren), Litton Ingalls Shipbuilding (Jim McIngvale and Bill Glenn), Raytheon Missile Systems (Colleen Niccum and Jennifer Spears), Defense Visual Information Center (Kathy Vinson and Connie Johnson), and the National Association of Destroyer Veterans (Tom Peltin). The latter organization, better known as Tin Can Sailors, Inc., provided me with a wealth of historical information and rare older photographs. I encourage destroyer aficionados everywhere to visit their Web site at www.destroyers.org. It's absolutely amazing.

And last, but not least, I would like to extend special appreciation to Vanessa Kostic at Kodak and Gary S. Rosenfeld at Fujifilm for supporting this book project by graciously providing technical advice and film. Based on their recommendations and test data, I ended up relying heavily on Kodak E200 professional film and on Fujichrome Velvia and Provia. As you can see from the results in this book, the right film makes all the difference in the world. All images I photographed were taken exclusively with Nikon camera bodies outfitted with a variety of Nikkor and Tokina lenses.

CHAPTER ONE

All spruced up for a change-of-command ceremony, the USS *Milius* (DDG-69) prepares to receive her new skipper. The photograph clearly shows the graceful-but-stealthy lines of this destroyer class. Notice how the superstructure aims skyward, the mast leans, and the bow and stern abruptly arc, all in an effort to make the destroyer as invisible as possible to enemy radar. The ship is even painted with a special gray paint to reduce its infrared signature. *S. F. Tomajczyk*

WEREWOLVES OF THE HIGH SEAS
The Destroyer Revolution

Among all of the ships found in the U.S. Navy's arsenal, there are very few whose title immediately grips your imagination. Aircraft carrier? Sounds like a Greyhound bus for planes. Cruiser? Either a police car or someone driving at a safe and steady 55 miles per hour. Submarine? How about a sandwich?

However, mention the word "destroyer" and an immediate association is one of power, blazing guns, streaking missiles, and smoke rising from the rubble. DESTROYER. It is synonymous with absolute destruction. Considering the fact that modern destroyers can be armed with nuclear-tipped cruise missiles, absolute destruction of the world as we know it is within the destroyer's capabilities. Yet destroyers are the harbingers of peace, not war. It is the threat of the possible use of their lethal weapons that resolves conflicts between nations and restores and maintains peace.

The lead ship of the class, USS *Arleigh Burke* (DDG-51), is shown under construction at the shipyard in Bath, Maine, in the late 1980s. This photo reveals the egg-shaped dome mounted on the bow that houses the ship's powerful SQS-53C sonar. Claimed to be the most advanced surface ship sonar in the U.S. Navy, it is a high-power, long-range system that can detect, identify, and track multiple surface ships and submarines at great distances. *Bath Iron Works*

Over the past century, destroyers have achieved a reputation and glamour that no other warship has equaled. They are sleek, hard-working, high-speed vessels whose role in naval surface warfare has quickly metamorphosed from undertaking just one task to becoming an all-purpose ship responsible for escorting the fleet, hunting down and sinking submarines, attacking the enemy with torpedoes and missiles, landing troops, or bombarding targets ashore. They are so indispensable in modern warfare that no aircraft carrier battle group (CVBG) will consider heading to sea without several destroyers for protection against enemy ships. In fact, a CVBG of 12 ships typically includes 3 or 4 destroyers, while larger battle groups include as many as 6.

Although the destroyer has been referred to in the past as the "Greyhound of the Sea" due to its nimble 30-plus knot speed, some military enthusiasts think the designation Werewolf is much more appropriate. When a crisis occurs, a destroyer transforms from a mild-mannered naval vessel into a swift and dead-serious warship armed with long, sharp teeth and claws. Twenty-four hours a day, seven days a week, destroyers stalk the high seas around the world keeping evil at bay.

The Birth of Destroyers

The destroyer dates back to 1870 when an engineer by the name of Robert Whitehead approached the British Admiralty with a new weapon he hoped would change the face of naval warfare. He built a vehicle that could travel the length of two football fields at a turtle's pace of 6.5 knots underwater. More noteworthy than speed was the guncotton warhead. All that had to be done was aim it at an enemy ship and the warhead would travel in a straight line and explode on contact with the hull. Whitehead named the device torpedo, after a type of tropical fish, the electric ray that stuns its prey.

The Admiralty was suitably impressed with the torpedo's capabilities and purchased rights to the weapon. Seven years later in 1877, the British launched the HMS *Lightning*, a small, newly designed warship armed with a single bow-mounted launch tube for a Whitehead torpedo. The *Lightning* fired the torpedo by accelerating to about 19 knots, steering herself at the target, and launching the weapon. The 14-inch-diameter torpedo had been modified to travel up to 600 yards at 18 knots.

The British ordered 19 of these so-called "torpedo boats," 8 of which were used for further experimentation. Because the ships were too small, narrow, and light to be deployed in heavy seas, they were restricted to defending harbors. Whenever an enemy ship threatened to blockade a harbor or attack a ship at anchor, one or more torpedo boats would sprint out of the harbor and launch their torpedoes.

In spite of their limitations, navies around the world were quite electrified with the torpedo boat—recognizing that it could destroy the largest warships with a single shot. Navies began to design and build their own variations, and soon torpedo boats could be found in Austria, Chile, France, Greece, Germany, Italy, Japan, and Scandinavia.

As this proliferation took hold, the British became quite nervous. They realized at some point in the future it was quite likely they

The *Arleigh Burke*-class destroyer USS *McFaul* (DDG-74) fires a Standard surface-to-air missile from its forward Vertical Launch System (VLS) during sea trials. Each destroyer has two VLSs: one fitted with 29 missiles that is mounted forward of the bridge, and one mounted astern containing 61 missiles. When a destroyer heads for sea, the VLS cells are filled with three different types of missiles: Tomahawks for precision land attacks, Standard missiles for aircraft, and ASROCs for enemy submarines. This mix gives the *Arleigh Burke* destroyers tremendous firepower. *Litton Ingalls Shipbuilding*

An SH-60 Seahawk LAMPS III helicopter refuels in flight from the USS *McFaul* (DDG-74) during a July 1999 training exercise in the Atlantic. This technique, referred to as a "hot pump" by sailors, enables the specially equipped helicopter to quickly return to its duty: searching for enemy submarines lurking in the area by using sonobuoys, a dipping sonar, and/or a towed magnetic-anomaly detector. *U.S. Navy*

could be at war with a nation who had dozens—if not hundreds—of torpedo boats at its disposal. How would they respond to the threat? Recognizing the answer was not to build more torpedo boats to match another nation's floating arsenal on a one-to-one basis, the Admiralty began to search for another solution.

Among the many proposals considered was the torpedo ram, an armored ship that had adequate speed to drive off torpedo boats, and had a reinforced ramming bow and

enough torpedoes of her own to go on to sink enemy ships. Although this concept sounded encouraging, the prototype proved to be a miserable failure. It was simply too slow to catch the lively torpedo boats.

Advancements often come from failure, and this particular instance was no exception. The British realized that the speed of larger warships had steadily risen since the mid-1870s and now they were only four knots slower than the torpedo boats. This meant that torpedo boats were vulnerable to naval gun fire. The Admiralty decided what it truly needed was a specially designed vessel with guns that could chase a torpedo boat, at the same speed or better, and sink her.

In 1887, four British Navy-designed torpedo catchers joined the fleet—the HMSs *Rattlesnake*, *Grasshopper*, *Sandfly,* and *Spider*. Unfortunately, in subsequent sea trials, these four ships proved unable to catch a torpedo boat unless the water was a flat calm. High-speed steam machinery was still in its infancy and, hence, unable to provide the power necessary for a catcher to decisively overtake a speedy opponent. Making matters worse, at maximum horsepower, the boats vibrated unbearably and threatened to come apart at the seams.

Throwing in the towel, the Admiralty finally sought the help of private torpedo-boat builders, correctly assuming they were the most likely people to be able to find an antidote to their own

An American medical-evacuation helicopter as seen through night-vision scopes during Operation Desert Storm. Night vision is routinely used by destroyers to detect and identify ships in the darkness. *U.S. Navy*

A CH-46 Sea Knight helicopter is carefully directed toward the flight deck of the USS *John S McCain* (DDG-56) during a vertical replenishment operation. *U.S. Navy*

Ever wonder what life at sea is like? Sailors say, "Buy a dumpster, paint it gray, and then live in it for six months straight." This photo demonstrates just how scarce space is aboard a destroyer. Sailors not only sleep stacked three high, but their clothing and personal belongings are stored in an 8-inch-high space that lies directly beneath their mattress and is locked shut with a padlock. *S. F. Tomajczyk*

product. A design request went out in 1892 for a "Torpedo Boat Destroyer." There were only two conditions that had to be met: a speed of at least 27 knots and a powerful gun armament.

The first prototype to appear was the HMS *Havock*, which underwent sea trials in October 1893. To the Admiralty's delight, the warship easily reached her designed speed of 26 knots and ran circles around torpedo boats she hunted down. As for armament, she carried one 76mm gun and three 47mm guns, as well as three 18-inch torpedoes that could be used to attack enemy ships. The shipbuilders envisioned the *Havock* destroying torpedo

boats with guns before moving in to attack the hostile main fleet as torpedo boats themselves.

Thrilled, the British Navy ordered 40 of these so-called 27 knotters, and quickly contracted to purchase 28 of an improved version that was in the process of being created, known as 30 knotters. The venerable and powerful destroyer was finally born.

The Destroyer Grows Up

Unlike other nations, the United States was slow to acquire torpedo boats. It was not until 1886—nine years after the British launched the HMS *Lightning*—that Congress was finally persuaded to build the first Whitehead torpedo boat, the USS *Cushing*. Launched in 1890, she had a top speed of 22 knots and displaced a mere 105 tons of seawater. Displacement is the weight (long ton) or volume (cubic meter) of a fluid displaced by a floating body and is the standard of how a ship's bulk is determined. In comparison, today's *Spruance*-class destroyers—named after World War II hero Rear Admiral Raymond Spruance—displace more than 8,000 tons fully loaded, and *Arleigh Burke*-class destroyers displace 10,000 tons.

Over the next six years, the Navy added 13 more torpedo boats to its fleet, just in time for the Spanish-American War of 1898. Although 6 torpedo boats were deployed for that conflict, no opportunity presented itself for the boats to attack the Spanish Fleet. For the lack of anything better to do, they went on patrol—a task that soon revealed their fragility and unreliability. Boilers burned out and pistons and valves jammed. Sailors were washed overboard in heavy seas and boiler room personnel were scalded to death by high-pressure steam. The living accommodations were cramped and inhumane, and the drinking water was often contaminated by rust and seawater.

These embarrassing faults spurred the Navy to make improvements to its torpedo boats. The timing could not have been better. The war with Spain loosened the necessary purse strings, allowing the Navy to not only

The USS *Russell* (DDG-59) leaves San Diego, California, for the Pacific Ocean and eventually back to Pearl Harbor, Hawaii, where it is homeported. To protect the ship's vulnerable (and expensive) 17-foot-diameter propellers from damage that might be caused by a careless tugboat skipper, the ship is equipped with cagelike metal guards on either side of the hull, positioned directly above the props at the waterline. *S. F. Tomajczyk*

purchase new torpedo boats but, more important, to quickly transition to the destroyer as other nations had already done.

Under the Navy's 1898 shipbuilding program, 16 destroyers were ordered. Four distinct types were constructed: three to private builders' designs, and one to blueprints drawn up by the Navy. Of these designs, the Navy's plans eliminated the traditional turtleback forecastle (pronounced "folk-sul") found aboard foreign ships and replaced it with a raised forecastle. This novelty was a tremendous improvement, making the destroyer more seaworthy. The ship's bow no longer easily buried itself into the waves, thereby allowing the ship to maintain its forward speed. Additionally, the raised forecastle offered better living space in the forward compartments and provided more work room for sailors working the ship's anchors and mooring lines.

Over the next century, the destroyer was constantly evolving to match the changes in naval warfare. The first major change was the introduction of the steam-turbine engine, which enabled the destroyer to travel at high speeds. This meant destroyers could escort and protect large battle groups and merchant convoys from hostile surface ships.

The *Fletcher*-class destroyer USS *Nicholas* (DD-449) as seen in the western Pacific in May 1967. She was one of three such destroyers that underwent a modernization overhaul. In this photograph you can see that a flight deck was added for the new Drone Antisubmarine Helicopter (DASH) system. In theory, the unmanned helicopter would be sent out using radio control signals to drop torpedoes on a submerged enemy submarine. In reality, the Drone often ran wild and flew upside down over its parent ship. Nearly 70 percent of all DASHs crashed. It was not until the late 1970s that the Navy finally placed ASW helicopters on its destroyers again, the LAMPS I. This photo also shows an early version of the Variable Depth Sonar (VDS) system. It is the pregnant-looking, torpedo-shaped device on the destroyer's stern. The VDS is trailed behind the warship at various depths and speeds to better detect lurking submarines. As for the USS *Nicholas* herself, she was one of America's most decorated destroyers. In fact, she was the flagship of the destroyer squadron that led the Allied fleet into Tokyo Bay in 1945. When she retired in 1969, she was the Navy's oldest active destroyer. *Tin Can Sailors, Inc.*

The start of World War I in the summer of 1914 also heralded the arrival of a plethora of new deadly weapons including the tank, chemical warfare agents, and submarine. It was the latter that directly affected the destroyer. German U-boats successfully blockaded Great Britain beginning in 1915 and stalked Allied convoys on the high seas, sending dozens of Allied ships to Davy Jones' locker, including the passenger ship *Lusitania*. Nearly 1,200 civilians perished in that incident, including 128 Americans.

At the outbreak of the war, no navy in the world had a warship specifically designed for antisubmarine warfare. That responsibility soon fell squarely on the shoulders of the destroyer. With her high speed, maneuverability, and shallow draft, the destroyer was the ideal makeshift submarine killer. She could sprint after an enemy submarine, following it into shallow waters if necessary, and then sink it. This was accomplished by the destroyer firing its deck guns at a submarine on the surface, or dropping depth charges on a submerged submarine. The depth charges were preset to explode at varying depths. The blast wave from the explosion easily buckled the sub's thin hull.

In 1917, the same year the United States entered World War I, destroyers were outfitted with hydrophones. This device enabled warships to locate submarines underwater by any noise they made, spurring the subs to "run silent, run deep." As a result, the threat posed by submarines was reduced for fear the submarines would be detected and destroyed. German submarine skippers knew what punishment was in store for them if they attempted to sink an Allied ship: hours and hours of depth charging, followed by gunfire if they tried to surface for air. It was a discouraging proposition, and Germany backed off.

World War II and Beyond

World War I ended in 1918 with the destroyer placed firmly atop a pedestal, admired by all the world's navies. No other warship had seen so much action or had as many physical changes. In the span of just a few years, the destroyer had metamorphosed from being a small, specialized craft into a warship that was an integral part of the fleet. As a result, naval architects ran to their drawing boards and began designing larger, more heavily armed destroyers in preparation for future wars and skirmishes.

Once again, the United States was the exception. It had a surplus of destroyers built between 1917 and 1922. It took the Navy eight years to convince Congress to fund any new destroyer construction. It was not until the 1930s that the Navy finally commissioned the *Porter, Mahan, Gridley, Somers,* and *Sampson* classes of destroyers. All of the warships incorporated advancements in propulsion, anti-aircraft weapons fire, and torpedo launch capabilities. For instance, the *Gridley*-class (1937) had four quadruple banks of 21-inch-diameter torpedo launch tubes. Carrying more torpedoes allowed the destroyers to remain at sea longer and fight the enemy.

In the late 1930s on the eve of World War II, the United States introduced the *Benson*-class destroyer. It displaced 1,620 tons and featured five 5-inch guns and 10 torpedo tubes. It was subsequently followed by the *Gleaves*-class

U.S. NAVY FLEET

As of 2000, the U.S. Navy Fleet comprises 313 warships. While that figure may sound impressive, it's actually not. Under the Reagan administration, the goal was to establish a powerful 600-ship naval force. Due to the collapse of the Soviet Union and the dissolution of a clear Communist threat to America, Congress ordered the downsizing of the Navy and the other military branches in the early 1990s. Unfortunately, with an increase in police actions and humanitarian aid missions in the 1990s and early twenty-first century, the Navy now finds itself stretched thin. Today, there is serious talk of increasing the size and capability of the naval fleet once again.

This chart provides you with an idea of the composition of the 313-ship fleet. Note that destroyers account for roughly 50 percent of the surface combatants and nearly 17 percent of the entire fleet. Obviously, destroyers are deemed a vital resource where naval warfare is concerned.

Aircraft Carriers	CV/CVN	11
Submarines	SSBN	18
	SSN	56
Surface Combatants	DD	24
	DDG	28
	CG	27
	FFG	27
Amphibious Warfare Ships		39
Combat Logistics Ships		34
Support/Mine Warfare		31
Active Reserves		18

Source: *Naval Vessel Registry*

The USS *O'Brien* (DD-725) plows through the warm Pacific Ocean somewhere between Pearl Harbor, Hawaii, and Yokosuka, Japan, in the spring of 1967. She is an *Allen M. Sumner*-class warship, and she appeared at the height of World War II in 1943, serving in the Atlantic Theater during the war. On June 25, 1944, she was providing cover for minesweepers operating off Cherbourg, France, when a German shore battery began firing at her. An 8-inch projectile hit the *O'Brien* near the signal bridge, detonating in the corner of the ship's Combat Information Center. All radars and one 40mm gun mount were put out of commission, and a fire broke out. Thirteen men were killed and 19 others wounded. In spite of the damage, the destroyer made it safely back to port, was repaired, and placed back in service. The *O'Brien* was finally stricken (no longer on active duty or in the Navy's inventory) in February 1972 and was later sunk that year as a gunnery target on December 1. *Tin Can Sailors, Inc.*

(1940) and by the *Fletcher*-class in 1942. The *Fletcher* class of 175 warships—with their excellent range, firepower, and seaworthiness—would prove to have one of the most successful all-around destroyer designs of World War II, with some remaining in service with the Navy until 1970. Measuring 376 feet long, *Fletcher*-class destroyers were armed with five 5-inch guns, three twin 40mm guns, several 20mm guns, and two quintuple banks of torpedo tubes amidships. The *Fletcher*-class was also the first to be equipped with a Combat Information Center (CIC), a room at the heart of the destroyer dedicated to analyzing data from radar, sonar, radio, and visual sightings. This information gave the captain a better picture of the battlespace around the ship and enabled him or her to make the best decisions in the heat of combat. The CIC has been incorporated into every destroyer class built since then, as well as into other surface warships.

While World War I was known for ushering in submarine warfare, World War II became famous for the shift from surface warfare to aerial warfare. From June 3 to 6, 1942, Japanese and American forces collided in the

South Pacific near a circular-shaped, 6-mile-diameter atoll known as Midway Island. This engagement, known as the Battle of Midway, marked the first time that two naval forces battled one another without their warships ever coming within sight of each other. The combat itself was exclusively fought by aircraft: propeller-driven fighters and bombers dueling it out over the Pacific Ocean.

The event sealed forever the aircraft carrier's future as the centerpiece of naval warfare, rather than the traditional and much-heralded battleship. Subsequently, destroyers were given a new responsibility: plane guard. In addition to escorting battle groups and merchant convoys, attacking enemy surface ships, conducting antisubmarine warfare, and laying down smoke screens for amphibious assaults, the destroyer was also expected to rescue downed American pilots who either crashed on takeoff from the aircraft carrier or were forced to ditch in the ocean. Rescuing downed pilots was a task destroyer crews readily took to.

The destroyer battles of World War II are among the more widely known of all destroyer battles. At Guadalcanal, 8 destroyers and 5 cruisers bravely took on 31 Japanese warships of the famed Tokyo Express. At Leyte Gulf—arguably the greatest sea battle in history—3 destroyers and 4 destroyer escorts fought the battleship *Yamato* in an effort to protect 6 unarmed transports from being sunk. At Okinawa, a destroyer picket line stood alone against Japanese kamikaze aircraft. Two destroyers were sunk and 7 others were badly damaged. The *Colhoun* was hit by 4 kamikaze aircraft before finally sinking. And at Cape St. George, Captain Arleigh Burke earned the nickname "31 Knot Burke" after he and three squadron mates of Destroyer Squadron 23 steamed to intercept and fight a convoy of five Japanese warships. The "31 knot" designation arose from Burke maintaining that speed, which was one knot faster than the maximum speed he had insisted his squadron could make while in formation.

By the end of the war in 1945, it was clear to military strategists that, once again, the face of warfare had dramatically changed. Signs of this were the arrival of the nuclear age with the bombing of Hiroshima and Nagasaki, the rapid advance of missile research and development, and air combat finally making the surface torpedo attack obsolete. Now, the enemy could be attacked from afar by aircraft, gunfire, and missiles. This point was underscored by the fact that of the 99 American destroyers lost during World War II, 49 were sunk by enemy air attack. The destroyer's thin hull plating, measuring a scant .125 inches thick, was easily penetrated by aircraft machine gun fire. In comparison, only 6 destroyers were sunk by surface-launched torpedoes.

All three of these developments significantly influenced the future of the destroyer. This became especially true in the postwar period as the United States grew increasingly leery of the intentions of the Soviet Union. Fearing an all-out Russian attack, the United States converted many of its destroyers into radar pickets. Equipped with powerful radar systems, the destroyers were sent far out to sea to provide the nation with greater early-warning time against incoming Soviet nuclear bombers.

During the course of the Cold War, which endured until the collapse of the Warsaw Pact and the Soviet Union in 1991, destroyers were modified to hunt down the more advanced and stealthy Russian submarines that carried nuclear ballistic missiles. The destroyers were outfitted with not only high-speed homing torpedoes, but also an arsenal of antisubmarine rockets.

To combat fighter jets, destroyers were initially equipped with rapid-firing 50-caliber guns that proved more effective than the older and slower 40mm guns. However, something more lethal was needed, since high-performance aircraft could launch guided missiles at a destroyer well beyond the reach of its 50-caliber guns. In 1956, the USS *Gyatt* (DD-712)—a *Gearing*-class destroyer—was

A rear view of the *Gearing*-class destroyer USS *Benner* (DD-805) as she steams through the Pacific Ocean in 1967. The *Gearing* class first appeared in 1944, and its ships were armed with six 5-inch guns, two 40mm twin anti-aircraft mounts, two 40mm quadruple anti-aircraft mounts, and two 21-inch quintuple torpedo tubes. In spite of the armament, these destroyers could sprint along at 34 knots. In this photo, you can see the *Benner* has a hangar and small landing pad (seen directly above the rear gun mount) to accommodate a helicopter—most likely the remotely operated (and unsuccessful) DASH helicopter system. The *Benner* was stricken in 1974 and disposed of as scrap in April 1975. *Tin Can Sailors, Inc.*

equipped with an experimental twin launcher that fired the Terrier anti-aircraft guided missile and had a range of 22 miles. The surface-to-air missile launcher replaced the ship's aft 5-inch twin gun mount. Although the *Gyatt* lacked proper missile fire control, she proved the feasibility of placing missiles aboard destroyers. Encouraged by the results, the Navy ushered in the *Charles F. Adams* class. The guided-missile destroyer—designated DDG—was born.

Today's Destroyers

Once upon a time—and not so very long ago—allied and enemy warships used to line up parallel to one another and fire hundreds of rounds until the opponent sank, surrendered, or scurried away. The reason they had to be so close to each other was because of the limited range of their weapons. During World War II, this distance measured a few miles at best. With the introduction of more-powerful guns and long-range missiles in the past three decades, however, a modern destroyer can fire and hit enemy targets well over the horizon and beyond sight.

The U.S. Navy has two classes of destroyers in service at the beginning of the twenty-first century: the *Spruance* class and the ultra-sophisticated *Arleigh Burke* class. Both destroyer types represent America's answer to today's current wartime threats in the world. Although the *Spruance* destroyers are primarily an antisubmarine warfare platform and the *Arleigh Burkes* serve in a multi-purpose combatant role, both are equipped to handle—at great distances—incoming missile attacks, enemy submarines, and hostile warships. They are also armed to launch and precisely deliver powerful cruise missiles against enemy targets located hundreds of miles inland.

At this writing, there are only 24 *Spruance* and 28 *Arleigh Burke* destroyers in service. These 52 destroyers represent roughly half of the 106 surface combatants at the Navy's disposal. The remaining surface warships are equally constituted of cruisers and frigates, while the rest of the fleet consists of aircraft carriers, amphibious ships, submarines, and support ships. (See sidebar on page 17)

The Navy organizes its destroyers into destroyer squadrons (DESRON). Years ago when the Navy had large numbers of destroyers on hand, DESRONs comprised solely destroyers. Now that the fleet is significantly smaller, however, DESRONs have been expanded to include frigates and, in five special cases, cruisers. Frigates are specially equipped to hunt down submarines—particularly in shallow waters—and to provide open ocean escorts for other warships and merchant vessels. The five cruisers assigned to three of the DESRONs are largely responsible for countering hostile air threats, which include enemy aircraft and incoming cruise missiles.

Elements of a destroyer squadron may be assigned to protect an aircraft carrier battle group against hostile forces or to conduct a variety of special operations, such as establishing and maintaining a maritime blockade, stopping ships suspected of transporting illicit drugs or other cargo, and escorting oil tankers through dangerous waters. The Navy also sends them to serve with North Atlantic Treaty Organization (NATO) naval forces that patrol the Atlantic Ocean (Standing Naval Forces Atlantic) and the Mediterranean Sea (Standing Naval Forces Mediterranean).

When an aircraft carrier battle group is deployed, it is always accompanied by ships of a DESRON, which are responsible for protecting the aircraft carrier from attack by enemy aircraft, submarines, and surface warships. While the battle group is commanded by an admiral, the elements of the DESRON are collectively commanded by a captain, who is addressed as Commodore and is often stationed aboard the aircraft carrier, reporting directly to the battle group commander.

The remainder of this book takes an in-depth look at both the *Spruance-* and *Arleigh Burke*-class destroyers. A better understanding of why destroyers are truly the "Werewolves of the High Seas" will develop as the book describes the ships' impressive fighting capabilities. Destroyers have not only metamorphosed over the past century in response to evolving combat threats, but they can also transform into a savage and lethal animal within seconds. It is no wonder that of all the different types of warships, the destroyer is the most feared.

DESTROYER SQUADRONS

Destroyer squadrons (DESRON) are the basic organizational units in surface warfare, and are generally composed of destroyers and frigates. The following chart provides you with a squadron's homeport, nickname, and its actual composition. Please note the actual number of each ship type assigned to a DESRON varies, and odd-numbered squadrons are assigned to the Pacific Fleet and even-numbered squadrons to the Atlantic Fleet.

Destroyer squadrons can be created (established) and retired (dis-established) as necessary. Since the official end of the Cold War in 1992—which reduced America's need to have destroyers constantly patrolling the world's oceans for enemy ships—many of the Navy's DESRONs have been dis-established. Although not currently in use, these same destroyer squadrons can be quickly established if a war begins, or if the Navy decides (with Congress' approval and funding) to add more ships to the Fleet.

In addition to the destroyer squadrons, this chart also lists the vertical launch cruisers assigned to the Navy's Carrier Group Commanders (CARGRU) and its Cruiser-Destroyer Group Commanders (CRUDESGRU). As mentioned earlier, the commander of an aircraft carrier battle group is always an admiral. By professional trade, he or she is either an aviator or a surface ship officer. When an aviator is in charge of a battle group, he or she is also given the title of Carrier Group Commander. Surface officers are given the title of Cruiser-Destroyer Group Commander.

Pacific Fleet
DESRON 1
San Diego, CA
"Total Force"
Naval Reserve Force: 5 reserve FFGs, No Destroyers
Curts (FFG-38), *George Philip* (FFG-12), *John A. Moore* (FFG-9), *Sides* (FFG-14), *Wadsworth* (FFG-9)

DESRON 7
San Diego, CA
"Golden Arrows"
Benfold (DDG-65), *John Paul Jones* (DDG-53), *Milius* (DDG-69), *Kinkaid* (DD-965), *McClusky* (FFG-41)

DESRON 9
Everett, WA
"On Guard"
David R. Ray (DD-971), *Paul F. Foster* (DD-964), *Fife* (DD-991), *Ford* (FFG-54), *Ingraham* (FFG-61), *Rodney M. Davis* (FFG-60)

DESRON 15
Yokosuka, Japan
"Champion of Freedom"
Vincennes (CG-49), *Curtis Wilbur* (DDG-54), *John S. McCain* (DDG-56), *Cushing* (DD-985), *O'Brien* (DD-975), *Gary* (FFG-51), *Vandegrift* (FFG-48)

DESRON 21
San Diego, CA
"Rampant Lions"
Valley Forge (CG-50), *Stethem* (DDG-63), *Higgins* (DDG-76), *Elliot* (DD-967), *Jarrett* (FFG-33), *Rentz* (FFG-46)

DESRON 23
San Diego, CA
"Little Beavers"

Decatur (DDG-73), *Fitzgerald* (DDG-62), *Hewitt* (DD-966), *John Young* (DD-973), *Oldendorf* (DD-972), *Thatch* (FFG-43)

DESRON 31
Pearl Harbor, HI
"Sea Warriors"
Hopper (DDG-70), *O'Kane* (DDG-77), *Paul Hamilton* (DDG-60), *Russell* (DDG-59), *Fletcher* (DD-992), *Crommelin* (FFG-37), *Reuben James* (FFG-57)

CRUDESGRU 1
San Diego, CA
Chosin (CG-65), *Lake Erie* (CG-70)
Note: These cruisers are homeported in Pearl Harbor, HI.

CRUDESGRU 3
San Diego, CA
Shiloh (CG-67), *Bunker Hill* (CG-52)

CRUDESGRU 5
San Diego, CA
Cowpens (CG-63)

COMCARGRU 3
San Diego, CA
Antietam (CG-54), *Princeton* (CG-59)

COMCARGRU 5
Yokosuka, Japan
Chancellorsville (CG-62), *Mobile Bay* (CG-53)

COMCARGRU 7
San Diego, CA
Lake Champlain (CG-57), *Port Royal* (CG-73)
Note: The Lake Champlain is from San Diego; Port Royal, from Hawaii.

Atlantic Fleet
DESRON 2
Norfolk, VA
"Second to None"
Arleigh Burke (DDG-51), *Mitscher* (DDG-57), *Porter* (DDG-78), *Deyo* (DD-989), *Stump* (DD-978), *Carr* (FFG-52)

DESRON 6
Pascagoula, LA
"Who Dares Wins"
Ticonderoga (CG-47), *Yorktown* (CG-48), *Thomas S. Gates* (CG-51), *John L. Hall* (FFG-32), *Estocin* (FFG-15), *Stephen W. Groves* (FFG-29)

DESRON 14
Mayport, FL
"Total Professionalism"
Moosebrugger (DD-980), *O'Bannon* (DD-987), *McInerney* (FFG-8), *Doyle* (FFG-39), *Robert G. Bradley* (FFG-49), *Samuel E. Morison* (FFG-13), *Boone* (FFG-28), *De Wert* (FFG-45), *Klankring* (FFG-42)

DESRON 18
Norfolk, VA
"Inimici Cavete" (Always on the Cutting Edge)
Stout (DDG-55), *Gonzalez* (DDG-66), *Nicholson* (DD-982), *Thorn* (DD-988), *Nicholas* (FFG-47)

DESRON 22
Norfolk, VA
"Facta non Verba" (Action not Words)
Cole (DDG-67), *Donald Cook* (DDG-75), *Caron* (DD-970), *Briscoe* (DD-977), *Hawes* (FFG-53), *Simpson* (FFG-56)

DESRON 24
Mayport, FL
"Keystone Squadron"
Carney (DDG-64), *The Sullivans* (DDG-68), *McFaul* (DDG-74), *Spruance* (DD-963), *John Hancock* (DD-981), *Underwood* (FFG-36), *Taylor* (FFG-50)

DESRON 26
Norfolk, VA
"Par Excellence"
Barry (DDG-52), *Laboon* (DDG-58), *Mahan* (DDG-72), *Arthur W. Radford* (DD-968), *Samuel B. Roberts* (FFG-58), *Kauffman* (FFG-59)

DESRON 28
Norfolk, VA
"Virium per Paratum" (Men through Preparation)
Ramage (DDG-61), *Ross* (DDG-71), *Peterson* (DD-969), *Hayler* (DD-997), *Elrod* (FFG-55), *Halyburton* (FFG-40), *Clark* (FFG-11)

CRUDESGRU 2
Norfolk, VA
Normandy (CG-60)

CRUDESGRU 8
Norfolk, VA
Anzio (CG-68), *Cape St. George* (CG-71)

CRUDESGRU 12
Norfolk, VA
Philippine Sea (CG-58), *Gettysburg* (CG-64)

COMCARGRU 2
Norfolk, VA
San Jacinto (CG-56)

COMCARGRU 6
Mayport, FL
Monterey (CG-61)

COMCARGRU 8
Norfolk, VA
Leyte Gulf (CG-55), *Vella Gulf* (CG-72)

COMNAVSURFGRU 2
Mayport, FL
Vicksburg (CG-69), *Hue City* (CG-66)

Sources: *Naval Vessel Registry and Naval Surface Force—Pacific Fleet*

CHAPTER TWO

A beautiful perspective of the sleek-looking USS *Spruance* (DD-963), the lead ship of the destroyer class that replaced the Navy's aging surface fleet, which up to then had consisted of the World War II-built *Gearing-* and *Sumner*-class destroyers. This photo reveals the *Spruance's* 61-cell Vertical Launch System mounted within the hull just forward of the bridge. It replaced two Armored Box Launchers (ABL), which held a total of eight missiles at any given time. A missile magazine located directly beneath the ABLs provided 16 reloads. As any destroyer skipper will attest, you can never have too much ammo. It's far better to have 61 missiles on hand than 24 when the fighting begins. In spite of her firepower, the *Spruance* is scheduled to be decommissioned in 2005, 30 years after entering service with the Navy. *Litton Ingalls Shipbuilding*

SPRUANCE DESTROYERS
Sleek Submarine Sinkers

Vietnam was not the only war the United States found itself fighting in 1972. Up on Capitol Hill in Washington, D.C., U.S. senators and congressmen were in an uproar. The appearance of a new type of naval destroyer being built in a Mississippi shipyard not only raised eyebrows, but heated up the voices lambasting the U.S. Navy for apparently wasting tax-payers' money. Critics judged the sleek-looking *Spruance*-class destroyer to be a bit *too* sleek looking!

Where are the weapons? demanded the congressmen, scanning the warship's uncluttered, near-barren gray decks. In stark contrast to Soviet warships at the time, which bristled bow-to-stern with sensors, guns, and torpedoes, the USS *Spruance* (DD-963) had only three visible weapon systems: two single-gun mounts and

A RIM-7 Sea Sparrow missile launches from the USS *Cushing* (DD-985) near Kauai, Hawaii, to intercept a drone from the Barking Sands missile range. This surface-to-air missile is used by *Spruance*-class destroyers to shoot down enemy aircraft within a nine mile radius. *U.S. Navy*

an antisubmarine rocket (ASROC) launcher. Considering the destroyers' size and expense, as well as the Soviet Union's growing military threat to America, critics cried foul play. What they failed to realize was that uncluttered did not necessarily mean inadequate.

Actually, these *Spruance* destroyers were extremely powerful warships. They were almost as well-armed as cruisers in close-in firepower, better equipped for surveillance and communications, and the best submarine hunters ever built. *Spruance* destroyers had an excellent mix of tactical weapons aboard with plenty of reloads, while the sensors, more sophisticated than those found on Soviet ships, required few and smaller antennas.

In an intense public relations effort the Navy had not anticipated the need for, senior officials countered Congress' angry accusations by pointing out that the state-of-the-art *Spruance*-class destroyer had been intentionally designed to hide its destructive power behind steel plates.

For example, the destroyer's six 12.75-inch torpedo launch tubes—three on each side of the ship—were concealed behind sliding doors. Likewise, the magazine for the ASROC launcher, containing 16 reloads, was hidden directly beneath it. These missiles could drop a high-speed homing torpedo or a 1-kiloton nuclear depth charge on an enemy submarine from up to 6 miles away.

Additionally, two Light Airborne Multi-Purpose System (LAMPS) helicopters were stored away inside a stern hangar. These specially equipped helicopters, carrying high-speed torpedoes, were designed to hunt down and sink submarines hidden over the horizon. The admirals insisted that while the "Spru-cans" appeared to be sleek and toothless, they were in fact lethal weapons. This machismo observation has been reaffirmed many times over since then. Today, if a *Spruance* destroyer appears off the coast of a hostile nation, its leaders look nervously seaward. No one wants to engage these sleek warriors.

Birth of the DX

At the height of the Cold War in 1966, the office of the Secretary of Defense realized the Navy needed to replace a large number of obsolete warships for carrier screening and fire support. Many of the surface combatants in the fleet at the time had been built for World War II, most notably the *Gearing-* (1943) and *Sumner-* (1944) class destroyers. Repair parts were increasingly difficult to find, which made overhauls long and expensive. The ships needed fairly large crews to operate, yet their spartan, Lilliputian living spaces discouraged sailors from re-enlisting; thereby jeopardizing the Navy's strength at sea. Adding insult to injury, submerged Soviet submarines could reportedly outrun many of the destroyers in heavy seas and were nearly invisible to older destroyers' sonar systems.

This distressing situation encouraged the Pentagon in 1968 to approach three shipbuilders to design a new class of destroyer, designated as "DX." In addition to outlining the surface combatant's required performance criteria (silencing, seakeeping, speed, range, and damage control), the Navy's project office stipulated the new warship had to displace less than 8,000 tons and be equipped with ASW sensors, weapons (including an armed helicopter), and guns for shore bombardment. It also had to be powered by gas-turbine engines rather than nuclear reactors to take advantage of the gas-turbine's power-to-weight ratio, responsiveness, and space conservation.

Two years later, the Navy selected Litton Industries' proposal for the DX because the

An SH-60B Seahawk conducts a helicopter in-flight refueling (HIFR) exercise with the USS *Connoly* (DD-979) during operation Support Democracy off the coast of Haiti. Known to sailors as a "hot pump," this refueling technique is used to decrease the time involved since the helicopter doesn't have to land, and ships without a flight deck cab refuel a helicopter in case of emergency. *U.S. Navy*

The USS *Oldendorf* (DD-972) is shown here docked at a pier in San Diego, California. *S.F. Tomajczyk*

company's shipbuilding philosophy favored large hulls and modular superstructures. This technique maximized the available space inside a ship and allowed it to be outfitted with machinery that was easy to maintain or replace. Litton's technique also allowed the destroyer to perpetually update its equipment with the latest high-tech weapon systems as they were developed. To upgrade a system, all that had to be done was simply remove the module in question and replace it with a new module containing the latest technology. By adopting this approach, the Navy hoped it would ensure that the *Spruance* class remained in front-line service throughout its expected 30-year lifetime.

Between 1972 and 1983, the Navy acquired a total of 31 *Spruance*-class destroyers, making it the largest shipbuilding project since World War II. All were built in Pascagoula, Mississippi, by Ingalls Shipbuilding, a subsidiary of Litton Industries. The lead ship, USS *Spruance* (DD-963), was launched on November 10, 1973, and commissioned on September 20, 1975.

Submarine Sinkers

The entire *Spruance* class was designed from the start for antisubmarine warfare to keep the Soviet Union's nuclear-armed submarine force at bay. To perform that mission, the destroyers were equipped with an integrated ASW combat system that could detect, locate, and track a submarine, and then assist in coordinating the launch of the ship's missiles and torpedoes to sink it. This state-of-the-art combat system relies heavily on two very sensitive sonar systems: a large bow-mounted sonar (SQS-53), and a passive towed array (SQR-19).

Claimed to be the most advanced surface ship sonar in the U.S. Navy, the SQS-53 is a high-power, long-range system that can detect, identify, and track multiple surface ships and submarines at great distances. The SQS-53 is mounted on the destroyer's bow in an enormous egglike dome crammed full of

576 transducers. The bottom part of this dome is rubber and floods with seawater when the ship is in motion, resulting in better power transference characteristics. Depending on the situation, the SQS-53 can be operated in an "active" or "passive" mode, or in both modes simultaneously.

In the active mode, a powerful sound wave is transmitted at a fixed frequency. Listening through headphones, sonar operators wait for the signal to bounce off an object, such as an enemy submarine, and return to the destroyer. A receiver attached to a computer measures the length of time between signal transmission and reception, and then calculates the

All the creature comforts of home: good food and television. Considering that a destroyer can be out to sea for as long as six months at a time, it has to provide the crew with good amenities and services. Otherwise, sailors would not re-enlist. As any skipper can tell you, a happy crew is a motivated crew that performs at its most professional level. *S. F. Tomajczyk*

Lieutenant Keith Moore (right) oversees the re-enlistment of CTR2 Michael Vaughn in the Navy. The brief ceremony took place aboard the USS *Oldendorf* (DD-972). Seaman Vaughn received not only a re-enlistment bonus but, more important, "chits" allowing him to sleep in from time to time. Upon completing his oath, Vaughn was congratulated by the ship's commanding officer, Commander Donald Babcock. *S. F. Tomajczyk*

Ensign Steven Susalla, the first lieutenant aboard the USS *Oldendorf* (DD-972), replaces the lifeboat roster at one of the many lifeboat stations on the ship. Each crew member is assigned to a specific lifeboat that he or she is to board in the event of an emergency. There are usually five to seven people per craft. In port, the rosters are changed daily to reflect the crew availability. Rosters are kept in waterproof "pill containers" affixed to the railing so that they are readily available. When the crew is ordered to abandon ship, the crew leader simply removes the list and reads off the names to ensure that everyone is present and not accidentally left behind. *S. F. Tomajczyk*

range (distance) and bearing (direction) of the object. Because sonar signals can be bent, scattered, or reflected by a host of uncontrollable environmental obstructions including the topography of the ocean floor, salinity differences, pressure gradients, and thermoclines (i.e., dramatic differences in water temperature at various depths), correctly interpreting sonar signals can be a difficult task for an operator. The good thing about using active sonar is that if there is anything nearby, the destroyer will quickly know it since there will be a distinct *ping* heard through the sonar operator's headphones.

The SQS-53 has three active sonar modes: surface duct, bottom bounce, and convergence zone. In the surface duct mode, the sound wave is transmitted in a horizontal plane, essentially parallel to the ocean's surface. This mode is used for relatively short distances since there is a high noise level in the return signal. In the bottom bounce mode, the sound wave is aimed at the ocean floor at an angle. The reflected energy is bounced upward from the floor toward the surface at considerable distances from the destroyer. Anything in the sound wave's path is detected.

The convergence zone mode takes advantage of the unique characteristics found in deep water. In this situation, the temperature, density, and pressure of the water affect the actual path of the sound wave—literally bending the sound wave's direction so that it surfaces again miles away from the destroyer in a "convergence zone." This mode provides the greatest range of coverage for the sonar when water conditions are favorable. The distance from a destroyer to the point where the convergence zone actually forms varies around the world. For instance, it is typically 15-plus miles in the Mediterranean Sea and 30 to 50 miles in the Atlantic Ocean. Again, anything

Opposite: Two sailors—electronics technicians Damon Phillips (bottom) and Anthony Anderson—go aloft to make some minor repairs to a radar system located on the ship's mast. For safety's sake they are constantly harnessed to the ship. *S. F. Tomajczyk*

SPRUANCE SPECS

Length	563 ft. (overall length); 528 ft. (water line)
Beam	55 ft.
Draft	32 ft.
Displacement	7,086 tons (light); 9,462 tons (fully loaded)
Engine	4 gas-turbine engines 80,000 hp (sustained); 86,000 hp (maximum)
Propellers	2, reversible pitch
Hull	Steel with aluminum superstructure
Speed	32-plus knots
Range	6,667 miles at 20 knots; 3,665 miles at 30 knots
Crew	24 officers and 272 enlisted personnel
Helicopters	2 SH-60B Seahawk LAMPS III
Missiles	2x4 Harpoon launcher (SSM)
	1x8 Mk 29 NATO Sea Sparrow launcher (24 total missiles carried)
	61-cell VLS (Tomahawk, Standard, and VLA)
	1 RAM (21 surface-to-air missiles)
Guns	2x1 5-inch (127mm) / 54-cal.
	2 20mm Phalanx CIWS
Torpedoes	2x3 Mk 32 12.75-inch torpedo launcher (14 total torpedoes carried)

Communications is vital in surface warfare, and the ancient art of signaling by color-coded flag has not been abandoned by the Navy. Unlike radio, it's a quiet form of communications that can only be seen by nearby ships. Since speed is everything in combat, signalmen must be able to "send" a message very quickly. This photo shows two sailors practicing their skill in port as an officer shouts out the message he wants to send. They are timed by stopwatch as to how quickly they raise (and lower) a message. *S. F. Tomajczyk*

in the sound wave's path is detected by the destroyer. Sonar operators monitor the sea conditions so they can anticipate how the convergence zone will be affected. As part of this effort, the ship drops expendable bathythermographs (XBT) into the ocean. These devices measure the sea's temperature at varying depths and indicate how sonar waves are bent by layers of warmer and colder water.

In its passive mode, the SQS-53 sonar system simply listens for noise being made by a ship or submarine, such as operating machinery or propeller cavitation. To prevent the destroyer's own noise from interfering with the sonar, the naval architects who designed the "Spru-cans" incorporated noise-suppression measures to keep the warships quiet, even when traveling at relatively high speeds.

Uh, I wouldn't stand there if I were you! But this sailor knows that and is simply humoring the author so he can get a photograph. These are blowout hatches for the destroyer's missile magazine. In the event of an explosion, the blast would be safely directed through these hatches and astern. Doing so minimizes the blast damage to the ship and its crew. *S. F. Tomajczyk*

Supplementing this submarine detection effort is the SQR-19 Tactical Towed-Array Sonar (TACTAS), which is stored in the Hoist Room—located under the ship's fantail—when not in use. The SQR-19 is essentially a very long cable towed behind the destroyer. At the end of the 5,600-foot-long cable is a linear array of hydrophones that passively listen to the ocean for sounds of underwater targets. This array, commonly referred to as the "noodle" or "tail," can be sunk to depths as low as 1,185 feet, and it can be operated in rough sea conditions up to Sea State 4 (8-foot-tall waves). How much cable is unwound depends on the desired ship speed and array depth. Acoustic data collected by the hydrophones, as well as information about heading, depth, and the water temperature, are continuously transmitted to the destroyer's ASW suite via a wire embedded in the tow cable. The entire sonar system weighs about 10,000 pounds.

When a submarine is detected, the destroyer has several options. If the ship's two sonar systems have done their job properly, the sub will be 20 to 100 miles away from the destroyer. In these circumstances, the destroyer typically launches one of its two LAMPS III helicopters. The helicopter flies out to the target area and drops sonobuoys into the water in a pattern that will entrap the submarine. Sounds detected by the sonobuoys are transmitted by radio frequency to the helicopter where they are analyzed and forwarded to the destroyer for further interpretation by computer and analysis by sailors in the ship's CIC. Once the sub's location is pinpointed, the helicopter then drops a high-speed, deep-diving Mk-46 torpedo into the water to pursue the sub and sink it.

If for some reason the destroyer's sonar systems do not do their job properly and, as a result, an enemy submarine is within a few

Crew training is never-ending on a destroyer, which is why the Navy has several Afloat Training Groups (ATG). Sailors from these groups visit ships around the world to provide hands-on training sessions to the crew. Here, David Kaiser (left) from ATG Pacific oversees the radio training of Jason Curry (right). *S. F. Tomajczyk*

miles of the destroyer, the destroyer's commanding officer may elect to launch an ASROC missile. Essentially a rocket-launched torpedo, an ASROC has a range of about 6 miles. It is fired from the warship's 61-cell Vertical Launch System (VLS), which is positioned ahead of the bridge. At a predetermined time after launch, the missile releases a homing torpedo to hunt down the submarine until it is destroyed.

SUCCESSFUL SPIN-OFFS

The flexibility of the *Spruance*-class destroyer's modular design impressed the Navy so much that it decided to use the same hull for the *Ticonderoga*-class guided-missile cruisers. These ships, with a price tag of $1 billion apiece, are optimized for the air-defense role with the powerful AEGIS combat system, as well as for the strike-warfare role with two 61-cell vertical launch systems.

The Iranian government was an ardent admirer of the *Spruance* destroyer. In 1974, the Imperial Iranian Navy placed an order for six destroyers. It requested, however, that the ships be optimized for the general warfare role rather than ASW. This meant adding two twin Mk 26 Standard surface-to-air missile launchers instead of the ASROC system.

When the Shah of Iran was overthrown in 1979 and replaced by a revolutionary government with an anti-American attitude, the export of the destroyers was embargoed. The U.S. Navy purchased the four ships already under construction for $1.353 billion and completed them as designed, making them the most powerful destroyers in the fleet at the time. These four modified *Spruance* destroyers were commissioned in 1981 and 1982, and officially became known as the *Kidd* class, although sailors often referred to them as the "Ayatollah class." The four ships in the *Kidd* class are USS *Kidd* (DDG-993), formerly Kouroosh; USS *Callaghan* (DDG-994), formerly Daryush; USS *Scott* (DDG-995), formerly Nader; and USS *Chandler* (DDG-996), formerly Anoushirvan. Like their *Spruance* sisters, the *Kidd* destroyers

were progressively upgraded over the years with Harpoon missiles, Phalanx CIWS, and LAMPS III helicopters.

The entire destroyer class was stricken in the late 1990s as a result of the Navy reducing the size of its fleet and replacing aging destroyers with the more modern, multi-mission *Arleigh Burke*-class destroyers. The USS *Chandler*, the last *Kidd* destroyer, was decommissioned in September 1999.

This is the *Ticonderoga*-class USS *Shiloh* (CG-67) launching a Tomahawk land-attack cruise missile during Operation Desert Strike. *U.S. Navy*

As a last resort, a destroyer will rely on its own arsenal of Mk-46 torpedoes to sink a submarine. There are three launch tubes hidden behind sliding doors on both sides of the ship's superstructure. The doors, which are located astern and below the helicopter deck, snap open and the torpedoes are fired at an angle away from the destroyer. Once they hit the water, they use active/passive acoustic homing to locate the hiding submarine and hunt it down, zipping along at an impressive 40-plus knots.

Theoretically, the last scenario should never happen. Today's submarines are quite capable of launching an attack against a surface ship from miles away. Hence, there is no reason why the submarine should be so close to a destroyer. However, with the Navy operating more often in shallow, confined bodies of water, such as the Persian Gulf, close encounters are becoming more of a reality. In spite of this, any destroyer skipper will be quick to tell you that the ASW weapon of choice is the torpedo hanging on the underside of a LAMPS III helicopter, because it can attack a hostile submarine over the horizon.

"The further away I can start the prosecution and kill him, the happier I am," confesses CDR Roger Coldiron, commanding officer of the USS *Stump* (DD-978). "If I have to rely on my torpedo tubes, I know I'm in serious trouble."

Ring of Steel

Because of the *Spruance*-class destroyer's highly developed weapon systems, it can hunt down and sink high-speed submarines in all weather conditions, and also engage ships, aircraft, and shore targets. This multi-mission capability enables the destroyers to operate either alone or as an integral part of an attack force. In the latter role, "Spru-cans" routinely find themselves protecting aircraft carriers at sea so the carriers are not attacked by missiles fired from enemy submarines or aircraft.

When it comes to projecting military power around the world, the aircraft carrier

Since the *Spruance* hull was also used in the *Ticonderoga* and *Kidd* classes, it can be difficult to tell whether the ship is a cruiser or destroyer from first glance. To make the identification easier, remember that destroyers have a boxy superstructure with 20 windows across the bridge. Cruisers have an angular superstructure that shrinks as it goes upwards and has nine windows across the bridge. Cruisers also have two flat and distinct AEGIS radars on its superstructure. If a ship is too far away, then rely on its hull number. Spruance destroyers are numbered 963 to 997, and the *Tico* cruisers are numbered 47 to 73. *Kidd*-class destroyers are all decommissioned so you can't confuse them with anything currently on the water. This photo is of the USS Cape St. George (CG-71) moored at the Norfolk Naval Base in Virginia. *S.F. Tomajczyk*

The engine control room aboard the USS *Oldendorf* (DD-972). *Spruance*-class destroyers were the first major warships in the U.S. Navy to be gas-turbine powered. Each ship has four gas-turbine engines—the same engines used to power jumbo jet aircraft, except with special marine modifications. They have start-up times measured in minutes and produce 80,000 sustained horsepower to give the ship a speed in excess of 32 knots. (FYI: One engine can propel the ship at 19 knots, two at 27 knots.) The use of these engines also helps the ship's sonar systems; they are much quieter than previous power plants. *S. F. Tomajczyk*

is universally acknowledged as the queen of a naval force. Yet, in spite of its tremendous size and the dozens of lethal fighters it carries on its flight deck, an aircraft carrier still never heads to sea alone. With few weapon systems of its own, the carrier is essentially defenseless. Hence, it must rely on the warfighting capabilities of a destroyer squadron to protect it.

A typical carrier battle group of 12 ships includes at least 3 or 4 destroyers—a mix of *Spruance* and *Arleigh Burke* warships—to serve as bodyguards. In some cases, there may be as many as 6 destroyers in the group.

"Carriers don't go anywhere without us," says CDR Coldiron. "They need the protection. When you're sitting on a carrier, it makes you feel a lot better to look out the window and see

a cruiser and destroyer around, especially if the air wing is off on a mission."

When an aircraft carrier is deployed, it is encircled by warships in a "Ring of Steel." The surface combatants—a collection of destroyers, frigates, and cruisers—are distributed to establish an enormous protective zone around the carrier. The size and shape of this zone constantly changes to accommodate emerging situations. As a rule of thumb, most zones in open ocean have a diameter of about 250 miles. The actual placement of warships within this zone is made by the battle group commander, who bases his decision on each ship's fighting or sensing capabilities, and by the direction of the threat, whether real or perceived.

Due to the *Spruance*-class destroyers' sophisticated ASW capabilities and powerful

Lunch time in the Chief's Mess (a.k.a. Goat Locker) aboard the USS *Oldendorf*. As everyone in the Navy knows, the chiefs have the best food. That's because they are the ones who run the ship and keep things on an even keel. Hence, the cooks tend to reward the chiefs with a bit more "tender loving care" where the food is concerned. Contented chief petty officers stay off your back—until you burn their favorite meal. *S. F. Tomajczyk*

Commander Donald Babcock, skipper of the USS *Oldendorf* (DD-972). At sea, he is an ever present figure in the bridge. That's because the ultimate responsibility for the safety of his ship and its 296 crew members is his, and his alone. If anything goes wrong, it's on his hands. More than one CO has found his naval career sunk after accidentally running a ship aground. *S. F. Tomajczyk*

gas-turbine engines that provide explosive sprinter's speed, they are generally positioned farthest away to detect and hunt down any lurking enemy submarines. Depending on circumstances, the distance can range from 20 to 50 miles from the aircraft carrier. While this may sound absurd, it is, in fact, prudent for two reasons. First, modern submarines can launch supersonic cruise missiles at an aircraft carrier from well over the horizon. In circumstances like this, distance is an ally. The faster a destroyer detects and shoots down the missile, the greater the chances are of the carrier's survival.

Second, the sonar systems found aboard a *Spruance* destroyer are more sensitive when the ship is positioned far away from the main body of the battle group. Any closer, and churning propellers from the dozen ships steaming through the ocean could deafen a destroyer's sonar system to the point where it couldn't hear a submarine "burning rubber" 10 feet away.

Tin Ears

Not every weapon found aboard a *Spruance*-class destroyer contains high explosives

Two gunner mates work on the USS *Oldendorf's* stern 5-inch gun, giving its barrel a protective coating to thwart saltwater's degenerative effects. When a destroyer deploys, it carries 600 rounds of ammunition for each gun. The magazine is located directly below the gun and is accessible from the open door you see on the gun mount. The mount's rounded angles were designed to help scatter enemy radar. *S. F. Tomajczyk*

Opposite: When a destroyer is in port, it receives a new coat of paint to reduce the effects of aging. Here, two sailors learn the fine art of painting a hull from BM2 Reginald Snipe, who is seated comfortably in the skiff. One sailor uses a gaff to keep the skiff close to the ship's hull while the other quickly applies the paint with a roller. As easy as it sounds, it's not. Each time the roller is moved up and down, the force propels the skiff away from the ship. These sailors almost landed in the drink several times. *S. F. Tomajczyk*

When the *Spruance* class first appeared in the 1970s, congressional leaders were angered by the ships' sleek, uncluttered look, as demonstrated in this photograph. Unlike destroyers before it, the *Spruances* simply didn't look dangerous enough to prevent a war from starting, much less end a war. But looks are deceiving! This is one lethal weapon capable of launching cruise missiles, antisubmarine rockets, torpedoes, and anti-aircraft missiles. According to the Navy, the cost to operate a single *Spruance*-class destroyer is about $35 million a year. *S. F. Tomajczyk*

or a nuclear warhead. In fact, it can be argued that a destroyer's most powerful implement of war is not its guns or missiles, it's the communications intelligence (COMINT) equipment. That is because accurate and timely information can often decide the outcome of battle well before the bullets fly. Knowing what the enemy intends to do, as well as where and when, allows U.S. military commanders to take appropriate actions and gain the upper hand on land and at sea.

Heeding the adage that "knowledge is power," the Navy equipped 16 "Spru-cans" in the 1970s with the SSQ-108 Organizational

Unit Tactical Baseline Operational Area Radio Detection (OUTBOARD) countermeasures exploitation system. Originally placed aboard two Navy cruisers in the 1960s, OUTBOARD is essentially a high-tech hearing aid that passively detects, locates, and identifies radio communications from sources located miles away and over the horizon.

The actual capabilities of OUTBOARD are classified, but it is known that the manually operated system enables a *Spruance* destroyer to park beyond sight off the coast of a foreign nation and listen in to what the enemy is doing. By monitoring communications, the

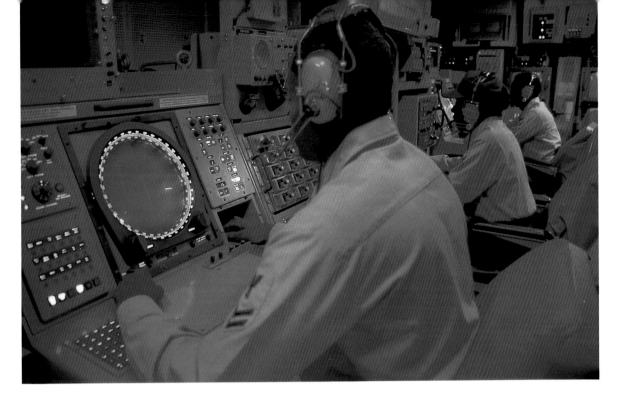

This is "Tracker Alley" aboard the USS *Stump* (DD-978), which is one component of the destroyer's Combat Information Center (CIC). The three radar operators shown here in Tracker Alley are responsible for tracking airborne targets—planes and missiles—near the destroyer. The blue lighting enhances the radar "blips" on the screen. As for the CIC, it is the heart of the ship where all combat sensor-related information flows for analysis and response. To ensure that the CIC survives an enemy attack, it is hidden deep within the bowels of the ship. *S. F. Tomajczyk*

Navy can learn many things, such as where command centers, military airports, and missile launch sites are located, as well as where surface ships are anchored. They can also learn of troop movements and preparation efforts for military deployments. Additionally, they learn the identities of senior commanders, and become familiar with daily military routines and what problems have arisen in the enemy's command and control structure.

At sea, OUTBOARD allows a "Spru-can" to secretly tail enemy warships and monitor their activities without being seen. Through this effort, the destroyer can gather accurate first-hand information regarding the capabilities and operations of the deployed hostile ships. The intelligence can help answer a slew of questions that may be nagging senior Navy commanders, such as: What is the purpose of this battle group? How are the combatants actually deployed within the battle group's protective zone? What evasive maneuvers do the ships take to prevent submarine or missile attack, and when? How well trained are the ships' crews? How long does it take for the warships to refuel under way? What encryption systems are they using to protect their radio communications? And what warships should our naval forces target for attack if war actually breaks out, and where exactly are they located within the battle group? What enemy sailors say to one another on the radio can answer these and many other important questions.

As for the OUTBOARD system itself, it comprises a VHF Adcock direction-finding antenna mounted atop the destroyer's forward mast and 24 small deck-edge antennas that intercept and determine the direction of lower frequency signals. According to electronic warfare experts, the antennas "vacuum up" the electromagnetic spectrum for communication signals—encrypted or not—that appear to be related to military activities. When a signal is intercepted by OUTBOARD, the system cannot only analyze it for content, but it can also determine where it came from. It does this by calculating the lapse in time it takes for the signal to be detected by at least three of the 24 shipboard antennas. Doing this triangulation results in the destroyer knowing the direction and range to the source.

Over the years, the Navy has taken advantage of OUTBOARD, using its spy capabilities to successfully wage military operations against Libya, Grenada, Beirut, and Iraq. The USS *Caron* (DD-970) was involved in both the 1981 and 1986 Gulf of Sidra incidents with Libya. Circumstantial evidence suggests she was also involved in the capture of the four Palestine Liberation Front terrorists who hijacked the SS *Achille Lauro* in 1985. Tailing the cruise ship at a safe distance, the *Caron* reportedly used her OUTBOARD system to listen in on the terrorists' radio communications, and then alerted officials as to their intentions.

Not everyone was as thrilled with the capabilities of OUTBOARD as was the U.S. Navy. In 1988, a Soviet *Mirka II*-class light frigate (FFL-824) in the Black Sea intentionally rammed the USS *Caron* to disrupt her surveillance efforts. The collision damaged the stern of the *Spruance* destroyer. Although the United States protested the incident, insisting the warship was exercising its right of free passage, the Kremlin retorted that the "Spru-can" had illegally entered the Soviet-claimed 12-mile territorial waters and had ignored the frigate's demands to leave the area. Only those who were there know what really happened and they are still not talking.

As with all technology, OUTBOARD has become antiquated since it first appeared on the *Spruance* destroyers more than 25 years ago. In 1995, the Navy began upgrading it with the Ships Signal Exploitation Equipment (SSEE). SSEE increases a destroyer's ability to detect, identify, and locate modern signals, which are faster and more condensed, at greater distances. SSEE, a manual system, constantly scans all communication frequencies and can pinpoint a source to within three degrees.

Sadly, *Spruance* destroyers will not receive the next generation of communications intelligence equipment because the destroyers will start heading for the scrap yards in 2005 with the lead ship USS *Spruance* (DD-963) being the first to decommission. Instead, the new Cooperative OUTBOARD Logistics Update (COBLU) will be placed aboard *Arleigh Burke* Flight II destroyers (DDG-72 onward) and on some *Ticonderoga*-class cruisers beginning in 2001.

COBLU is a joint United States and United Kingdom venture that began in 1994. It significantly builds on the capabilities of the original OUTBOARD system, and is designed to operate in environments where there is a very dense communications flow. Using advanced digital technology, COBLU will be capable of automatically recognizing current and new signals of interest in all communication bands simultaneously. According to one electronic warfare expert, COBLU will be able to do this by comparing intercepted signals with an enormous database of signal types previously collected by America's intelligence community, including the super-secret National Security Agency. Analysis of the signals will be done at lightning speed, literally a nanosecond or two, thereby giving warship commanders near-real-time information about what the enemy is doing. This becomes vitally important when a destroyer or aircraft carrier battle group suddenly finds itself in the enemy's crosshairs.

After having been at sea for six months, the USS *Stump* (DD-978) undergoes repairs at the Norfolk Naval Base. Over the next several months, it will receive upgrades to its sensors and weapon systems, as well as a paint job. It will also take on some new crew members. Following that, it will participate in several training exercises to hone its fighting edge so that the *Stump* can go back to sea for another six months. *S. F. Tomajczyk*

Millennium Warrior

Throughout history, the destroyer has constantly metamorphosed to successfully counter advancements in warfare. The *Spruance*-class destroyer is no different. It underwent a dramatic change in the 1980s, transforming from a dedicated ASW platform to more of a multi-purpose combatant. One instigator of this change was the Cold War between the United States and Russia. Senior Pentagon officials anticipated waging an enormous and bloody war in the middle of the Atlantic or Pacific Ocean with the Soviet Navy—battle group against battle group. This meant there was no room in the U.S. fleet for

ships that could perform only one specialized task. Instead, multi-purpose warships able to respond to anything thrown at them—bullets, missiles, or torpedoes—were needed.

It was the development of the Tomahawk anti-ship cruise missile (TASM) in the late 1970s that enabled the *Spruance* destroyers to actually transform into multi-purpose combatants. This new missile represented a major development in naval warfare. Rather than a missile flying in a straight line to its target, which usually took evasive measures to avoid being hit by the incoming missile, TASM skimmed along the ocean's surface until, at a predetermined distance, it began an active radar search to detect, acquire, and destroy the enemy ship. In other words, the cruise missile could maneuver in response to anything the enemy did, thus ensuring a direct hit.

After extensive sea trials in 1981, the USS *Merrill* (DD-976) in October 1982 became the first U.S. surface ship to ever carry TASM. The destroyer was outfitted with armored box launchers (ABL) for eight TASM cruise missiles. With a range of 220 miles, a speed of 550 miles per hour, and a 1,000-pound high-explosive warhead, TASM dramatically enlarged the battlespace. Now an enemy ship could be easily sunk without a destroyer ever having to confront it in person. It was the perfect weapon for waging a sea battle against Soviet naval forces.

TASM was quickly accompanied by a land-attack version, known as the Tomahawk Land Attack Missile (TLAM). Designed as a long-range, all-weather cruise missile, TLAM enables a destroyer to accurately attack enemy targets located hundreds of miles inland from

IN THE HEAT OF COMBAT

Spruance-class destroyers have earned a reputation for being at the heart of a fight. During Operation Desert Storm in 1991, *Spruance* destroyers fired more Tomahawk cruise missiles than any other ship type. Five destroyers of the *Spruance* class launched 112 Tomahawk missiles at Iraqi targets. The USS *Caron* launched 2, the USS *Fife* launched 60, USS *Leftwich* fired 8, the USS *Foster* launched 40, and the USS *Spruance* fired 2 missiles. These missiles represented 39 percent of all the Tomahawk missiles fired during the Gulf War. The USS *Paul F. Foster* earned the distinction of firing the first Tomahawk and, hence, the opening salvo of the war on January 17, 1991.

During the conflict, several *Spruance* destroyers served as floating airports for a detachment from the Army's elite 160th Special Operations Aviation Regiment (aka Nightstalkers) and its two OH-58D Kiowa Warrior light-attack night helicopters. These small attack helicopters were used to recapture Kuwaiti islands held by Iraqi military forces. They were vectored to and from their targets by an embarked Navy SH-60B helicopter that used its surface-search radar.

During Operation Desert Fox in December 1998, American warships, including the USS *Nicholson* (DD-982), conducted a 70-hour attack against Iraqi targets to reduce Saddam Hussein's ability to make weapons of mass destruction. The Navy launched more than 300 Tomahawk missiles, depleting 10 percent of its inventory.

And last, during Operation Allied Force in March 1999, battle group surface combatants located in the Adriatic Sea launched the opening Tomahawk salvo against targets in Yugoslavia. Again, the USS *Nicholson* participated in this mission by launching TLAMs.

A gunner's mate aboard the USS *John Young* (DD-973) loads a 70 pound projectile into the 5-inch gun as the ship operates in the Persian Gulf in February 1998. The two single-barrel guns provide gunfire support to Marines ashore as well as limited anti-ship and anti-air coverage. *U.S. Navy*

the ocean. The missile uses an internal computer map to determine where the missile is by comparing the surrounding terrain with the map. If necessary, the missile can automatically adjust its bearing to get back on the correct, preprogrammed course to the target. The TLAM is an extremely accurate weapon and is capable of delivering either a conventional or nuclear warhead against a hostile target 600 to 1,000 miles away, depending on its payload.

While the Tomahawk ABLs were being retrofitted on seven *Spruance* destroyers, a naval engineer came up with the ingenious idea of storing and launching the missiles vertically. Doing so allowed a warship to carry more missiles in the same amount of space. For example, 61 Tomahawk missiles could be stored in the same space occupied by the two ABLs that held only eight missiles. The point was crystal clear, and 24 of the *Spruance* destroyers received the Mk 41 VLS. The seven destroyers that did not get the VLS upgrade were decommissioned in 1998. Installing the VLS meant ripping out the existing ASROC launcher and magazine positioned forward of the ship's bridge, but it was worthwhile.

Today, the VLS is found aboard all in-service *Spruance* destroyers. Capable of launching Tomahawk, Standard, and ASROC missiles, the VLS enables a destroyer to hit the enemy hard from phenomenal distances.

"Unlike bomber and attack aircraft that often need to be forward-deployed in a foreign nation, we don't need anyone's permission," points out destroyer Captain CDR Roger Coldiron. "We're a launch basket in the middle of the ocean, in international waters. When the order comes, we simply fire our Tomahawks."

The Tomahawk missiles he is referring to are the land-attack variants (TLAM). After briefly experimenting with the TASM, the anti-ship type, the Navy decided to remove them from all surface ships and put them in storage. In their place, warships now rely on the sea-skimming Harpoon missile to attack hostile ships. In fact, all *Spruance*-class destroyers

A gunner's mate aboard the USS *Leftwich* (DD-984) retrieves a spent 5-inch shell casing from the ship's forward gun. Each *Spruance* destroyer has two single-barrel guns: one mounted on the bow and the other on the stern. The magazine for each gun is located directly below the mount and holds 600 70-pound shells. *U.S. Navy*

today are equipped with two Harpoon launchers, each of which holds four missiles.

Other improvements made to the *Spruance* destroyers include the addition of the NATO Sea Sparrow surface-to-air missile; Recovery Assist, Secure, and Traverse (RAST); the Rolling Airframe Missile (RAM); and radar-absorbent material throughout the ship's exterior. Other improvements also include the installation of LAMPS III electronics that allows an SH-60B LAMPS III helicopter to send ASW data in near real-time to the destroyer, and the placement of Kevlar ballistic material in all vital, internal areas of the ship to provide additional protection for the crew from spalling, bullets, and fragmentation.

CHAPTER THREE

USS *Ross* (DDG-71) sails in the Gulf of Mexico during one of her predelivery sea trials. *Litton Ingalls Shipbuilding*

ARLEIGH BURKE CLASS
Stealthy Sea Ghosts

When people first step aboard an *Arleigh Burke*-class destroyer, they are immediately struck with the sense that they must be either drunk or in a fun house. That, or the ship builders were drunk when they built the ship. Why? Everything on the destroyer is crooked. There is not a straight and vertical piece of steel anywhere! Bulkheads tilt away from you, and the superstructures are bent and faceted. The ship's tripod mast leans precariously backwards, the deck curves abruptly skyward at the bow and stern, and the railings are diamond shaped.

Sailors aboard these destroyers use the "Banana Split Sundae" analogy to describe their warship to civilians: "Take a banana, turn it crest side up, and then top it with lots of triangular-shaped goodies. That's an *Arleigh Burke*. Don't bother trying to eat it, though, because you can't eat what you can't find."

The USS *Fitzgerald* (DDG-62) cuts a sharp but graceful turn in the ocean. Although the destroyer's top speed is classified, the Navy acknowledges that it is in excess of 31 knots. Sailors mutter in awe about the ship being able to kick up a "rooster tail" when traveling at 35 knots. During Operation Desert Fox in December 1998, the *Fitzgerald* raced at top speed for three days from the Indian Ocean to reach its launch position in the Persian Gulf. It arrived on the last night of the operation, with only 14 percent of its fuel remaining, and was able to launch eight Tomahawk missiles at Iraqi targets. *U.S. Navy*

And finding it is indeed the trick. An *Arleigh Burke* destroyer is the Navy's equivalent of the Air Force's F-117 Nighthawk stealth fighter. It is designed bow-to-stern for extreme stealth on the high seas, enabling it to thwart hostile naval forces and, in turn, destroy the fleet with lethal weapon systems. The class is arguably the most powerful ever put to sea. These guided-missile destroyers perform a variety of missions, including anti-air warfare, anti-surface warfare, and antisubmarine warfare.

Sea Ghosts

While the *Arleigh Burke* destroyers are built around the AEGIS combat system and SPY-1 radar, they were also designed from the start for stealth and survivability. After all, a warship that can be easily detected and sunk by the enemy is useless, regardless of what powerful weapon systems it can bring to a fight.

To make the destroyer more invisible to hostile forces, marine architects cloaked the ship in stealth technology. The architects reduced the destroyers RCS by avoiding flat, vertical surfaces. Anything that went on the ship had to trap, degrade, or bounce incoming radar waves in a harmless direction so that the enemy would have a difficult time pinpointing the ship's location. Hence the superstructures were faceted, funnels were angled, hand railings were diamond shaped, and all bulkheads were tilted skyward or at the ocean's surface. Even the deck of the ship was abruptly angled at the bow and stern to redirect radar from an enemy plane back into the sky, collapsing the radar wave on itself in the process. Additionally, special radar-absorbent foam was affixed to any curved surface that might cause radar spikes. This included such things as the tripod mast, external fuel pipes, and bulkhead corners.

The overall result was a destroyer with the radar signature of a small, nonmilitary type vessel—an amazing feat. More than once, an *Arleigh Burke* destroyer's RCS has lulled hostile forces into a false sense of security, incorrectly believing the "blip" on their radar screen to be a fishing boat when, in fact, it is a heavily armed destroyer.

As for survivability, these warships are the first since World War II to have steel hulls and superstructures. This decision was made primarily as a result of a tragic naval accident that occurred on November 22, 1975. The guided-missile cruiser USS *Belknap* (CG-26), collided with the aircraft carrier USS *John F. Kennedy* (CV-67) near Sicily during the night. The USS *Belknap* was severely damaged, with its superstructure essentially sheared off. A fire broke out and the aluminum bulkheads began to melt. In the end, 8 sailors were killed and 46 others were wounded. The incident taught the Navy that aluminum and warships were a poor combination where safety was concerned.

The all-steel construction of the *Arleigh Burkes* (with exception to their funnels and mast, which remain aluminum) provides increased resistance to flying fragments, fire damage, and the blast pressure created by a missile or mine detonating near the ship. The

Anyone have marshmallows? A Tomahawk land-attack cruise missile, surrounded by its fiery plume, is launched from the *Fitzgerald's* forward vertical launch system. This is one of the eight missiles the destroyer fired at Iraqi targets during Operation Desert Fox. Upon returning to homeport, used missile cells are unbolted and removed from the VLS, and then replaced with another missile canister. *U.S. Navy*

The USS *Roosevelt* (DDG-80) is gently nudged free by a tugboat from an Ingalls floating drydock during her first launch on January 10, 1999. She is the second Flight IIA to be built for the Navy, and features a helicopter hangar aft that can accommodate two LAMPS III antisubmarine warfare helicopters. The *Roosevelt* was commissioned in October 2000. *Litton Ingalls Shipbuilding*

addition of 130 tons of bulletproof Kevlar armor plating to vital areas of the ship (bridge, engine room) helps ensure the crew's safety and the ability of the destroyer to continue to operate after being struck by enemy weapons fire. All accommodation compartments are equipped with sprinkler systems.

To further ensure survivability, the ship's Combat Information Center (CIC)—the nerve center of the ship where all combat-sensor information flows—is located within the hull, surrounded by passageways. Likewise, the sonar room is placed well forward, away from the CIC. If the CIC is damaged by a hit, the sonar room will hopefully still be intact for operation.

As for the durability of the destroyer's electronics, the data-processing architecture is distributed to ensure that the ship's weaponry cannot be disabled by a single hit. Furthermore, all critical systems are shielded against electromagnetic pulse, an intense but short-lasting

ATTACK ON THE USS *COLE*

Nothing is indestructible. The truth of this vulnerability was demonstrated on the morning of October 12, 2000, in the port of Aden, Yemen when the USS *Cole* (DDG-67) was attacked by terrorists as it refueled.

The *Cole*, carrying a crew of more than 300, had left Norfolk, Virginia, on August 8, and was heading for the Persian Gulf to participate in maritime-interception operations being conducted there. The destroyer stopped in Aden to do a quick 5-hour refueling before continuing on into the Arabian Sea.

The most current timeline of the attack at the time of this writing shows that the USS *Cole* arrived at one of the port's offshore berths at 8:30 A.M. and began to tie-up with assistance from harbor tugs and line-handling boats. At 9:05 A.M., additional small craft, including food and garbage collection boats, arrived. The *Cole* completed its mooring operations around 9:30 A.M. and began to take on fuel at 10:30 A.M. from a floating refueling barge located on the ship's starboard side. The destroyer had been refueling for about 45 minutes when, at 11:18 A.M., a small, explosive-laden boat pulled alongside the *Cole* and detonated. Allegedly, the boat's two operators stood proudly at attention as they came along side, as if anticipating the blast.

The powerful explosion ripped through the *Cole's* half-inch-thick steel hull, and opened a 30-by-40-foot hole at the waterline. The destroyer's number one main engine room and an auxiliary engineering compartment immediately flooded, and caused the warship to list 4-degrees to port. The explosion also tore through the crew and chief petty officers' mess and galleys. Had the ship's captain, CDR Kirk Lippold, not ordered all hatches below-deck closed and dogged before the *Cole* entered the harbor, the destroyer would have likely sunk.

Seventeen sailors were killed and 39 were wounded. It was the most deadly terrorist attack against the US military since June 1996 when a truck bomb killed 19 Air Force personnel living in Khobar Towers in Dhahran, Saudi Arabia.

The horrific terrorist attack at Aden illustrates the potential hazard Navy personnel face on a daily basis, whether in time of war or peace. In an interview with *Navy Times*, Seaman Apprentice Andrew Nemeth, a 19-year-old gas turbine technician who was injured in the attack, said, "We weren't really told about any dangers, but being in the Navy you expect it. Anytime you go into the Persian Gulf, you know something might happen."

Although the Aden-Abyan Islamic Army claimed responsibility for the attack on the USS *Cole*, an investigation led by the FBI suggests that Osama bin Laden's global network of terrorists was ultimately behind it. Officials say the nature of the attack itself indicates that the bombers were well-financed, intelligent, and had sophisticated logistics.

In the aftermath of the bombing, the U.S. Navy signed a $4.5 million contract with the Norwegian firm Offshore Heavy Transport to transport the USS *Cole* to the United States aboard the heavy-lift ship, *Blue Marlin*. The *Cole* was positioned at an angle so its large bow-mounted sonar dome hung over the side of the *Blue Marlin*. The Navy estimates it will cost $150 million to repair the *Cole*. The four-year-old destroyer cost about $1 billion to build.

The *Winston S. Churchill*, which will be hull number 81 when commissioned by the Navy, is launched at Bath Iron Works on April 17, 1999. A lot of work needs to be done to the ship before it is handed over to the Navy for sea trials, including the addition of the powerful, egg-shaped SQS-53C sonar on the bow. It can take one to two years after launching before a ship is actually commissioned. At that time, it receives its official "USS" designation and is manned by a crew. *Bath Iron Works*

A beautiful overhead view of an *Arleigh Burke*-class destroyer at sea. You can clearly see the ship's angular construction, as well as the flight deck (an incoming helicopter aligns itself with the diagonal line), 61-cell VLS, Mk-32 torpedo launchers, rear CIWS, and the forward 5-inch gun. Also take note of how wide the ship is. Unlike other destroyers that are generally 10 times longer than their width, the *Arleigh Burke* destroyers are only 7 times longer. This gives the ship greater stability at sea, while maximizing the internal hull space. *Bath Iron Works*

Crew members of the USS *O'Kane* (DDG-77) maintain the Navy tradition of running aboard to bring the ship to life during the ship's commissioning ceremony at Pearl Harbor on October 23, 1999. The destroyer is named after Medal of Honor winner Rear Admiral Richard H. O'Kane, skipper of the submarine USS *Tang* during World War II. *U.S. Navy*

The USS *Stout* (DDG-55) returns to port at the Norfolk Naval Base after conducting training exercises at sea. The Navy has spent a considerable amount of money in the past decade to retrofit surface ships such as the *Stout* to accommodate female crew members. To do this to *Arleigh Burke* destroyers, it cost $1.4 million per ship. By comparison, it cost $2 million per *Nimitz*-class carrier and a mere $700,000 for each *Ticonderoga*-class cruiser. *Arleigh Burke* destroyers typically have a total crew of 346, 48 of them women (6 officers, 6 chief petty officers, and 36 enlisted). *S. F. Tomajczyk*

Seaman Eric Silverberg is laughing now, but that's because it's still early in the day. A few hours spent over the side of the USS *Fitzgerald* (DDG-62) chipping paint off the hull under the hot San Diego sun may dampen his enthusiasm. The strange-looking device in his left hand is a needlegun, which strips the paint off metal. *S. F. Tomajczyk*

Fire controlman Jason Phipps of the USS *Fitzgerald* (DDG-62) checks to make sure the CIWS is properly loaded with dummy ammunition. The bright yellow-colored plastic shells are inserted when a ship is in port. Similar-colored plastic caps are inserted into the tips of the Gatling-style barrels to prevent rain and sea spray from causing rust. *S. F. Tomajczyk*

electric and magnetic field that is produced by a nuclear explosion. These short pulses of high current, which move away from the blast, are capable of disrupting or even destroying sensitive electronic equipment, computers, communications gear, and radar and sonar systems.

And last, every destroyer is outfitted with the Collective Air Protection System, that protects the ship's crew from nuclear fallout and chemical and biological warfare agents. The *Arleigh Burke* class represents the first warship ever to possess this technology. The destroyer has double air-locked hatches and fewer accesses to the weather deck, thereby reducing the risk of contamination. The interior of the ship is also slightly overpressurized so that if the hull or superstructure is somehow penetrated, fallout and contagion are unable to enter. Additionally, all incoming air is heavily filtered and emphasis is placed on recirculating the air within the ship to prevent contamination from the outside air.

Above: The USS *Russell* (DDG-59) heads for sea. From this angle, you can clearly see two of the ship's four SPY-1 antennas mounted on the superstructure. Each covers a 90-degree sector from the horizon to the space directly over the ship. The SPY-1 is the most powerful radar in service with any navy in the world. Its extremely complex signal structures prevent it from being jammed by enemy countermeasures, and it can cut through sea clutter to detect small radar cross section, sea-skimming missiles. The *Arleigh Burkes* are currently outfitted with the SPY-1D version, but a more advanced antenna, the SPY-1D(v), is due to be retrofitted on Flight IIA destroyers beginning in 2003. *S. F. Tomajczyk*

Right: Seaman apprentice James Dymond uses a needlegun to clean the wire cable used to lower one of the USS *Fitzgerald's* two rigid-hull, inflatable boats (RHIB). The RHIB has a V-shaped fiberglass hull to offer stability and a rigid motor mount, along with an inflatable gunwale section made from neoprene and nylon-reinforced fabric. This design makes the craft very tolerant of heavy seas. The destroyers use them to send a boarding party over to a cargo vessel it has stopped in international seas. *S. F. Tomajczyk*

The Shield of Zeus

The USS *Arleigh Burke* (DDG-51) was commissioned on July 4, 1991. Named after Admiral Arleigh Burke, arguably the most famous naval officer to lead a Destroyer Squadron into battle during World War II, it was the lead ship of a revolutionary class of guided-missile destroyers. The *Arleigh Burke* was a smaller warship compared to traditional destroyers and was designed to use an improved sea-keeping hull, reduce infrared and acoustic signature, and have a smaller radar cross section (RCS). By having a smaller RCS, it meant the ship reflected very little of the enemy's radar waves back to the source, making the destroyer appear to be a fishing boat on the enemy's radar screen instead of a warship. Simply put, all of the new characteristics made the *Arleigh Burke* more stable and more difficult for the enemy to find at sea.

Above: One of the nice things about being in port is that when the day is done, you can go ashore to be with your family or paint the town red. In this photo, take note of the diamond-shaped railings and the radar-absorbent material wrapped around the pipes to the right. Both enhance the ship's stealth capabilities. Also, the color purple (top right) is used to designate that something has a fuel function. In this case, it's apparently a fuel line. *S. F. Tomajczyk*

Right: No, it's not a twenty-first century phone booth. It is the flight control room aboard the USS *Fitzgerald* (DDG-62). From here, an incoming helicopter is given landing directions to the flight deck. The strange gold-green tint to the glass is a special material embedded into the glass to scatter enemy radar waves. It is found on all the windows in the ship's bridge as well. *S. F. Tomajczyk*

Welcome to the dark world of the USS *Fitzgerald's* CIC, located deep within the ship's hull to ensure its survival in the event of an enemy attack. Data from all the ship's sensors are routed to the CIC for real-time analysis. At the heart of this room is the AEGIS combat system, which detects and tracks targets, and then coordinates an attack against them. The control panel shown in this photo is where the commanding officer and tactical action officer sit to review the combat information presented on the screens in front of them. *S. F. Tomajczyk*

The *Arleigh Burke*-class can trace its beginnings to the 1960s when the Navy anticipated an all-out war with Russia that would involve the launching of hundreds, if not thousands, of missiles. To handle this type of saturation attack, the Navy developed the AEGIS combat system.

Named after the mythological shield of Zeus, the Greek god of the heavens and the earth, AEGIS is an anti-air warfare system that unites a warship's computers, radars, and missiles to provide an enormous defensive umbrella over the ship itself or over an entire aircraft carrier battle

Even though the *Arleigh Burke* destroyers are completely made of steel (excluding their aluminum funnels and mast), the crew must still be prepared to fight a fire at sea since other things on the ship *do* burn. Hence, fire drills are conducted on a routine basis, with the fire crews timed in their response efforts. Here, a three-man fire crew responds to a fake helicopter crash on the *Fitzgerald's* flight deck. Note the use of the self-contained breathing apparatus to prevent smoke inhalation. *S. F. Tomajczyk*

Left: Commander James S. Grant, CO of the USS *Fitzgerald* (DDG-62), sits in the skipper's chair on the bridge. He and his crew participated in Operation Desert Fox, launching eight Tomahawk missiles against select Iraqi targets to reduce Saddam Hussein's ability to produce weapons of mass destruction. In his cabin, he keeps a piece from one of the Tomahawk's casing as a reminder of that eventful evening. The *Fitzgerald* earned its third "Battle E" award in March 2000, signifying that it is the best ship in DESRON 23. *S. F. Tomajczyk*

Opposite: A look at the front 5-inch gun and the 29-cell VLS positioned behind it, as well as the CIWS mounted below the bridge. *S. F. Tomajczyk*

Every day aboard a destroyer begins with the ship's executive officer (XO) briefing department heads about the work plan of the day. After asking questions and clarifying issues, the department heads in turn inform their staff and the work day begins. *S. F. Tomajczyk*

group. The system automatically detects and tracks numerous airborne, seaborne, and land-launched targets simultaneously, and coordinates the firing of the ship's various weapons at them. At any given moment, AEGIS can track more than 100 targets.

The very first AEGIS system was tested in 1973 aboard the USS *Norton Sound* (AVM-1), an aging guided-missile ship. Its subsequent success encouraged the Navy to place the combat system aboard cruisers using the hull and machinery design of *Spruance*-class destroyers and adding a vertical launch system (VLS). While this approach worked, it quickly became clear to senior officials that

the AEGIS-equipped, *Ticonderoga*-class cruiser was too expensive to continue building and too difficult to backfit with new technologies.

That's when the *Arleigh Burke* class was sketched out on paper. It was envisioned as being a smaller and cheaper version of the AEGIS cruisers, and its entire design was focused on the AEGIS combat system and the SPY-1, a powerful multi-function phased-array radar that can detect enemy targets as far away as 250 miles. Unlike traditional radars, which are curved and rotate, the SPY-1 antennas are flat and fixed. A 12.5-foot-wide radar "face" is mounted on each of the four corners of the ship's superstructure, angled at 45 degrees.

Prior to the development of the SPY-1, ship radars mechanically rotated atop a mast. The radars scanned a target when the radar beam struck the target during each 360-degree rotation. A separate tracking radar was then used to engage the target. In contrast, the SPY-1 integrates these functions. The four octagonal-shaped antennas each transmit 4,480 precise beams of energy simultaneously in all directions to detect, track, and engage dozens of missiles and aircraft, while continuously watching the sea and sky for new threats. Each antenna covers a 90-degree quadrant from the horizon to the space directly overhead, creating a virtual radar bubble around the ship.

Control of the SPY-1 is done by four computers that schedule and direct the individual radar beams. This is necessary because the SPY-1 projects thousands of pencil-thin beams in a lightning-fast sequence—far too complex for a human operator to do. When an aircraft or missile is detected, the computers automatically order several beams to linger on the target, thereby beginning a track. The SPY-1 determines the range and bearing of the target, its speed, and classification (missile or aircraft type). The data is constantly updated and sent to the AEGIS combat system that coordinates the firing solution for the Standard (SM-2) surface-to-air missiles carried by *Arleigh Burke* destroyers. The missiles are stored within two Mk-41 vertical launch systems: a 29-cell positioned forward of the bridge, and a 61-cell located astern.

When an SM-2 is launched, the SPY-1 continuously tracks both the missile and the target. If necessary, the missile's guidance system can be updated electronically from the ship while in flight, but generally, specific radar guidance is needed only during the last few seconds before the missile detonates to make sure it hits the target.

During the past decade, the Navy has invested more than $350 million in a series of improvements to enhance the AEGIS system's theater missile defense capabilities, as

Fire controlman James Isenman receives the Navy Achievement Medal from Lieutenant Commander Mike Sparks, the *Fitzgerald's* combat system officer. The medal is presented to Navy personnel who distinguish themselves by meritorious service or achievement. Since this was also Isenman's last day aboard the destroyer before shipping off to a new assignment, he was additionally given a framed photograph of the ship, signed by his shipmates. *S. F. Tomajczyk*

For the incoming skipper, the change-of-command ceremony is an eagerly awaited event in his or her life. All officers aspire to be the CO of a warship. This is also why the ceremony is dreaded by the outgoing skipper: he or she is likely heading for a desk job somewhere. The Navy likes its officers to have a well-rounded background at sea *and* ashore. In this photo, the USS *Milius* (DDG-69) dresses up to receive her new commanding officer. *S. F. Tomajczyk*

well as its ability to detect incoming anti-ship cruise missiles that fly a few feet above the ocean's surface.

Heart of the Beast

The CIC is where all combat-sensor information flows for analysis and response. It is hidden in the bowels of the ship to ensure its survival in the event of an enemy aircraft strafing, missile explosion, or an underwater mine detonation. It is staffed around the clock to detect hostile targets and quickly coordinate the ship's offensive (or defensive) efforts.

When you step into the CIC, the first thing you notice is that it is a dark and chilly room, eerily lit with pale blue lights. Additionally, it is a cramped room filled with consoles and workstations that glow with fluorescent ruby, tangerine, and lime green buttons and monitors. The entire visual effect, accompanied by a constant electronic hum of the powerful computers, makes you feel as if you are in a *Star Wars* epic movie.

In the center of the CIC are three large AEGIS combat-display monitors. They colorfully and graphically show what is transpiring everywhere within 250 miles of the destroyer. This information is posted in near real-time. The ship's Tactical Action Officer (TAO), and in wartime, the Commanding Officer, will be in the CIC watching the monitors to see what is happening in the surrounding area.

On one monitor, for example, an overhead view of the destroyer's location is shown with all targets (ships and aircraft) clearly identified. With a simple click of a computer mouse, the TAO can zoom in on a particular target and gather data about the target's range, heading, and speed in relation to the destroyer. If the target is an aircraft, its IFF code appears on the screen to identify whether it is a friendly or hostile aircraft. Positioned around the outer periphery of the CIC are various workstations that represent an aspect of warfare that is vital to the survival of the ship. These aspects include antisubmarine, surface, strike, air combat, and electronic warfare. These mini-command centers monitor the raw or processed data that is forwarded from the ship's individual sensors.

For example, in the ASW module, key data from the destroyer's SQS-53 bow-mounted sonar system and SQR-19 towed sonar array are displayed, including the identification of any sonar contacts by submarine class. This processed information is sent to the CIC from the Sonar Room located elsewhere in the ship.

Strike!

The CIC is where all the action takes place in a crisis. It is here where Tomahawk missiles are launched at targets ashore, Harpoon missiles are fired at surface warships, Standard missiles are fired at incoming enemy aircraft or cruise missiles, and antisubmarine rockets and torpedoes are launched at submarines. The CIC is a hectic place to be in times of war—especially when the AEGIS combat system and SPY-1D radar are at their maximum effort, monitoring and responding to more than 100 targets.

Although the *Arleigh Burke* destroyers missed Operation Desert Storm in 1991 because the class was not in service with the Navy at the time, they have participated in all naval operations since then. They have

A rare peek inside a VLS cell. A heavy-duty canister containing the missile is lowered into the cell and then bolted in place. Just beneath the protective green covering shown here is the tip of a Tomahawk land-attack cruise missile. When the missile is fired, the metal hatch swings open and then, a split second later, the missile rips through the protective covering and roars skyward. (Note that the green covering is scored with an "X" to facilitate this.) All the crew feels is a slight shudder. For those on the bridge, however, they can watch the fiery plume scorch through the sky. The event is especially spectacular at night. *S. F. Tomajczyk*

The USS *Oscar Austin* (DDG-79) became the very first Flight IIA destroyer when she was commissioned on August 19, 2000. Unlike earlier *Arleigh Burke* destroyers, she is equipped with an upgraded hull-mounted sonar system for mine detection and avoidance, and she boasts an improved AEGIS weapons system, *plus* (as shown in this photograph) two hangars for SH-60B Seahawk helicopters for enhanced surface attack and ASW operations. The state-of-the-art destroyer is named for Medal of Honor recipient Private First Class Oscar P. Austin who gave his life in Vietnam to save an injured fellow Marine. Appropriately, the ship's motto is "Honor and Sacrifice." *Bath Iron Works*

escorted oilers through the Persian Gulf, protected aircraft carrier battle groups on the high seas, intercepted foreign ships and inspected their cargo, and fired their weapons to enforce America's commitments and preserve peace overseas.

Among the destroyer's numerous weapon systems, the Tomahawk land-attack cruise missile (TLAM) is the one most often ordered and used by the National Command Authority consisting of the president and secretary of defense. The TLAM is a highly accurate weapon capable of striking a small target in a congested area from 800 miles away. As Navy officials boast, you can launch a TLAM from Virginia Beach, Virginia, and have it fly

Opposite: It's 0730 hours at the naval base in San Diego. Each morning at this time, the colors are proudly hoisted aboard every warship as officers and enlisted men alike snap to attention wherever they are standing. In the following silence, which lasts as long as it would take to play the national anthem, no one moves. This simple act pays tribute to the nation these sailors defend and honors the lives of those who have died in past wars and conflicts to preserve democracy and the American way of life. *S. F. Tomajczyk*

Two propellers, attached to four gas-turbine engines that produce as much as 100,000 horsepower, drive the *Arleigh Burke* destroyers at speeds in excess of 32 knots. The actual speed is classified, but sailors brag it's fast enough for the destroyer to throw a "rooster tail" of water behind it. Each of the controllable, reversible-pitch propellers has an enormous 17-foot diameter that dwarfs the workers in this photo. *Bath Iron Works*

through the goal posts at Soldier Field in Chicago, Illinois.

With Tomahawk-armed destroyers constantly patrolling the world's oceans as stealthy sea ghosts, they can precisely strike hostile targets, including those located hundreds of miles inland, with very little notice. This power projection capability has become known as Strike Warfare.

During Operation Desert Fox in December 1998, U.S. Naval forces—the USS *Stout* (DDG-55) and USS *Fitzgerald* (DDG-62) included—smashed Iraqi targets with more than 300 Tomahawk missiles. The assault lasted only 70 hours and significantly reduced Saddam Hussein's ability to build weapons of mass destruction. The *Fitzgerald* joined the attack at the last minute, having sailed at high speed for three days from the Indian Ocean to the launch site in the Persian Gulf. She managed to launch eight Tomahawks before the Operation ended.

Arleigh Burke destroyers also participated in Operation Allied Force against Yugoslavia in March 1999. The USS *Gonzalez* (DDG-66), along with other surface combatants such as aircraft carrier cruiser frigates, demonstrated the projected power of Tomahawks again. This time it complemented air strikes against a number of inland targets.

ARLEIGH BURKE SPECS

The *Arleigh Burke* class was constructed in flights, which allowed the Navy to add technological advancements to the ships during construction. Flight II ships (DDG 68–78), introduced in 1992, incorporated improvements to the ships' SPY radar and Standard missile, active electronic countermeasures, and communications. The Flight IIA ships (DDG-79 onward) are longer than earlier destroyers in the class—511 feet versus 505 feet—because they are equipped with a helicopter hangar to carry one ASW helicopter and one armed attack helicopter. Additionally, the Flight IIA ships have an upgraded hull-mounted sonar system for mine detection and avoidance.

Flight IIA Ships (DDG-79 onward)

Length	511 feet (overall length); 471 feet (waterline)
Beam	66 feet (max); 59 feet (waterline)
Draft	33 feet
Displacement	6,600 tons (light); 9,157 tons (fully loaded)
Engine	4 gas-turbine engines 90,000 hp (sustained); 100,000 hp (maximum)
Propellers	2 17-foot diameter controllable reversible pitch
Hull	Steel hull and superstructure with aluminum funnels
Speed	Classified (32-plus knots)
Range	4,890 miles at 20 knots
Crew	32 officers and 348 enlisted personnel
Helicopters	2
Missiles	2x4 Harpoon launcher (SSM) 90-cell VLS (Tomahawk, Standard, and VLA) 29-cell forward; 61-cell astern
Guns	1x1 5-inch (127mm) / 54-cal. Mk-45 2 20mm Phalanx CIWS
Torpedoes	2x3 Mk-32 12.75-inch torpedo launcher

The bridge superstructure of the USS *Fitzgerald* (DDG-62) is carefully lowered into place aboard the hull during her construction. The AEGIS SPY-1 flat radar antennas and all the ship's weapons and electronic warfare systems will be added later on. One interesting feature shown in this photo is the radical, flared bow. It is intentionally designed that way to bounce radar waves downward into the sea, thereby enhancing the warship's stealth characteristics. *Bath Iron Works*

As these records confirm, the *Arleigh Burke*-class destroyers are formidable fighters. This image was enhanced in September 1989 when the lead ship, the USS *Arleigh Burke* was launched at Bath Iron Works in Maine. Someone allegedly asked retired Admiral Burke, who attended the ceremony, how he would have liked having a destroyer like that back in World War II. Without hesitation, the famous destroyerman responded, "If I'd had a destroyer like this, there would've been no World War II."

CHAPTER FOUR

Destroyers typically carry two Mk-32 triple-tube torpedo launchers—one positioned on either side of the ship. When needed, the launcher rotates outward where the torpedo is then fired over the side into the ocean. The Mk-32 can launch both the Mk-46 lightweight torpedo and the Mk-50 advanced lightweight torpedo ("Barracuda"). Destroyer skippers consider the torpedo to be a last-ditch weapon against a submarine. Their preference is to attack a submarine *much* farther away using either a helicopter-dropped torpedo or an antisubmarine rocket. The Mk-32 launcher shown in this photo is aboard the USS *Fitzgerald* (DDG-62). *S. F. Tomajczyk*

FIREPOWER!
Destroyer Weapon Systems

Weapons are what give the destroyer its teeth and claws in combat. While the *Spruance* destroyers are known for possessing stronger ASW capabilities than the *Arleigh Burke* destroyers, both classes share similar weapon systems. What differs is the amount of firepower they are able to deliver in times of war.

At the heart of both destroyer classes is the powerful Mk-41 Vertical Launch System, which enables the warships to vertically store several different missile types, ready for immediate use. The VLS is actually embedded into the ship's hull so that the hatches at the top of the cells are flush with the main deck. A *Spruance* destroyer has one 61-cell VLS mounted forward of its bridge, while an *Arleigh Burke* destroyer carries a 29-cell on its bow and a 61-cell astern for a total of 90 missiles. The VLS is designed to launch any one of three types of missiles: the BGM-109 Tomahawk, RIM-66 Standard, and the RUM-139 Vertical Launch ASROC (VLA).

The USS *Fitzgerald* (DDG-62) (a.k.a. *Fightin' Fitz*) launches a Standard missile (SM-2) from its stern VLS, which contains 61 missiles. The SM-2 is the *Arleigh Burke* class' primary surface-to-air missile to defend against incoming enemy aircraft and cruise missiles. The fire-and-forget missile has a range of about 100 miles and travels at more than twice the speed of sound. A modified version of the Standard is being developed to shoot down short-range ballistic missiles; it will be carried and launched by AEGIS-equipped destroyers and cruisers. *U.S. Navy*

The Rolling Airframe Missile (RAM) is found aboard a handful of *Spruance*-class destroyers. It provides them with enhanced point-defense against incoming aircraft and missiles out to a distance of about 5 miles. Mounted on the ship's stern, RAM is arguably one of the most popular roosting spots on the destroyer for seagulls (when it's not being fired, of course). *Raytheon Company*

Tomahawk

The Tomahawk is the Navy's premier long-range, subsonic (550 miles per hour) cruise missile. After the missile is launched from a destroyer, a solid propellant rocket booster propels it until a small turbofan engine takes over for the cruise portion of the flight. The Tomahawk has a high survival rate because of its small radar cross section and its ability to fly at very low altitudes following an evasive flight path toward its target.

Destroyers are routinely armed with the Tomahawk Land-Attack Missile (TLAM), of which there are several different types. The Block II TLAM version uses a terrain comparison and digital scene-matching guidance system. As the missile flies toward its target up to 610 miles away, it uses an internal, digitized computer map to determine exactly where it is by comparing the surrounding terrain with the map. If necessary, the missile can adjust its bearing to get back on the correct course.

The Mk-41 VLS has dramatically changed the face of surface warfare. In the past, destroyers were constrained by how many missiles they could carry and fire at the enemy from a deck-mounted launcher. With the advent of VLS, which orients the missiles vertically and stores them within the ship's hull, a destroyer is now able to carry as many as 90 missiles instead of the traditional dozen or so. *Raytheon Company*

The current Block III TLAM adds Global Positioning Satellite (GPS) guidance capability to the terrain comparison and digital-matching efforts. This means that the missile receives constant navigation data from the Defense Department's 24 GPS satellites. The result is extreme accuracy. The missile remains roughly within 16 feet of its intended flight path.

The Tomahawk is a very versatile cruise missile. It is capable of carrying both nuclear and conventional warheads, as well as dispensing bomblets (as many as 168 armor-piercing, fragmentation, or incendiary bomblets) over a target area. The nuclear version of the Tomahawk (TLAM-N) has a 200-kiloton warhead and a range of 1,050 miles.

The Navy is now developing the Block IV Tomahawk, which should be operational in 2003. Known as the Tactical Tomahawk, it will carry a warhead filled with smart submunitions (bomblets that have sensing/homing capability). The missile can be reprogrammed in flight to strike any of 15 preprogrammed alternate targets, or it can be sent new GPS coordinates to hit another target.

Amazingly, the Tactical Tomahawk will also be capable of loitering over a battlefield for several hours after dropping a portion of its submunitions. As it flies over the area, it will transmit images via its on-board TV camera to war-fighting commanders so they can assess damage done to the target. If necessary, they can then direct the missile to re-attack the original target or move on to a new target.

Spurred by the success of the Tomahawk, the Navy is also developing a kinetic-energy variant of the Tactical Tomahawk, which will be equipped with a special penetrator warhead to attack buried enemy command posts and bunkers. It will be capable of plowing through several layers of dirt, rock, concrete, and steel before detonating deep underground.

Standard

The Standard missile is a medium-range surface-to-air and surface-to-surface missile used by *Arleigh Burke* destroyers and other AEGIS-equipped warships to protect themselves against enemy aircraft, ships, and cruise missiles. Launched from the ship's VLS, the SM-2 (MR) is a two-stage missile that features midcourse guidance and improved resistance to enemy jamming efforts. It has a range of about 45 to 100 miles and can hit targets flying at altitudes of 80,000 feet. It travels at speeds of Mach 2.5 and is equipped with semi-active radar homing (radar that turns on and off during the missile's flight to acquire the target) and a high-explosive warhead that has a proximity fuse that detonates the bomb when it reaches a certain distance, determined by radar, from the target. Each missile costs $421,400.

The extended-range version of the Standard—designated as SM-2 (ER)—has an inertial guidance system with semi-active homing radar and a high-explosive warhead. It can hit targets at distances of 75 to 115 miles.

The Standard missile has been so successful since it was first introduced in 1971 that the Navy is developing a modified, high-tech version to shoot down theater ballistic missiles. Known as the Standard Missile 2 Block IV, the new missile, equipped with an infrared

An unmanned BQM-34 Firebee target drone is launched off the USNS *Gosport's* weather deck. This drone, which was used to simulate enemy aircraft attacks, was launced high over the ocean where it was successfully intercepted by a Standard missile (SM-2) fired from the USS *O'Kane* (DDG-77). Firebees are routinely used to test a destroyer's ability to detect, track, and engage an enemy target. *U.S. Navy*

An unmanned BQM-74C target drone is given a final inspection prior to being launched from the USS *O'Bannon* (DD-987) during UNITAS, a combined exercise involving the naval forces of the United States and nine South American nations. The rocket-powered drone will be used as a target by anti-aircraft gunners aboard ships taking part in the exercise. The BQM-74C is ideal for simulating sea-skimming missiles, and is capable of emitting active radar signals to mimic certain types of missiles. *U.S. Navy*

The USS *Benfold* (DDG-65) fires its 5-inch gun during routines off of San Clemente Island. The gun can be automatically reloaded from its 600-round magazine below the deck while the gun is firing. The 70-pound projectile can fire at a target 16 miles away. *U.S. Navy*

seeker, proved its intercept capabilities when it destroyed an airborne Lance ballistic missile over White Sands, New Mexico, during testing in 1997. The Navy hopes to eventually field these missiles aboard AEGIS destroyers and cruisers to provide protection of seaports, coastal airfields, and allied expeditionary troops around the world.

Additionally, the Navy is in the process of modifying up to 800 SM-2 missiles (of both types) to the Land Attack Standard Missile configuration. It will serve as an interim missile aboard the *Arleigh Burke* destroyers until the Advanced Land Attack Missile (ALAM) is eventually deployed on the Navy's next-generation

destroyer, the DD-21 class. Chapter 5 provides more details about this stealthy warship.

Vertical Launch ASROC (VLA)

The VLA is considered to be a destroyer's primary antisubmarine weapon. It consists of a Mk-46 Lightweight homing torpedo strapped to a solid-propellant rocket motor. After the 16-foot-long missile is launched at a submarine, the booster is jettisoned at a predetermined point and the payload continues to follow a ballistic flight until a parachute deploys to gently lower the torpedo and its protective casing to the ocean. Upon entering the water, the protective nose cap breaks apart

Two fire controlmen load a chain of 20mm ammunition into the forward, Phalanx Close-In Weapon System (CIWS) mounted aboard the USS *John S. McCain* (DDG-56). At the time, the *McCain* was operating in the Persian Gulf in support of Operation Southern Watch, the enforcement of the "No Fly" zone over southern Iraq. The CIWS (pronounced "seewhiz") fires a high volume of rounds to create a wall of bullets the missile or aircraft has to fly through to reach the ship. The fully automatic, Gatling-style gun system is considered to be a "last ditch" effort at saving the warship from attack. *U.S. Navy*

and the parachute cuts free. The torpedo's motor starts and its homing sensors become active. It goes into a search mode to locate and attack the enemy submarine. Although the information is classified, the VLA reportedly has a range of about 6 miles.

The Navy also has a nuclear version of ASROC in its inventory. It has a 1-kiloton nuclear depth charge that is powerful enough to sink any submarine within a 3-mile radius. Unlike the conventional VLA, which uses a parachute to slow its descent, the nuclear warhead freefalls into the ocean and then detonates at a preset depth. As the Cold War thawed, the nuclear ASROC was withdrawn from active service in 1989, but it remains in the Navy's arsenal for future use.

Sinking the Enemy

In addition to the VLS, destroyers have other weapon systems available to them. One of the most important is the Harpoon, the Navy's principal anti-ship cruise missile. A subsonic, sea-skimming missile, the Harpoon is capable of striking enemy warships at distances in excess of 60 miles. Target data is fed into the Harpoon before launching, including over-the-horizon radar sources (stations,

A SH-60 Seahawk LAMPS III helicopter fires an AGM-119 Penguin anti-ship missile at a target ship during a naval training exercise. The missile hit the former *Knox*-class frigate just 24 inches above the waterline, sending it to Davy Jones' locker. LAMPS III helicopters routinely deploy with destroyers to provide expanded anti-submarine warfare capability. *U.S. Navy*

planes, surface ships, satellite systems), if available. Once launched, a radar altimeter maintains the missile's trajectory height.

Unlike some missile systems, the Harpoon does not have to be lined up with its target before being launched. Even if the Harpoon is fired in the opposite direction of the target, it is smart enough to turn around in flight and attack it.

As the Harpoon approaches the target, an active-radar terminal seeker searches and locks on to the enemy warship commanding the missile to abruptly pull up and swoop in on the vessel from above. This maneuver is designed to outsmart any defensive weapons the warship may have, such as a Gatling-style gun or anti-missile rocket. The missile's capabilities are so impressive and reliable that the Navy takes the following attitude about it: "Find the Enemy. Fire a Harpoon. Pick up survivors."

The silhouette of the USS *John F. Young* (DD-973) sails by a pair of Iranian command and control platforms in the Persian Gulf that were set on fire after being shelled by four U.S. Navy destroyers. The shelling was in response to an Iranian missile attack on a reflagged Kuwait supertanker. *U.S. Navy*

There are four versions of the Harpoon, the most notable being the RGM-84D. It enables the missile to re-attack the target by flying a clover-leaf pattern if it fails to acquire the ship on the initial approach. It also has a larger fuel tank than the earlier models, nearly doubling its range from 88 to 166 miles.

The Navy is currently developing a new type of Harpoon missile, Harpoon Block II, which will enable destroyers and other surface combatants to attack enemy vessels in coastal and shallow water regions of the world. This missile will use the military's GPS system to pinpoint targets in difficult-to-reach areas, such as ships anchored close to shore or hidden in small coves. If all goes well with the missile's research and development efforts, it will be available in 2001.

Another noteworthy anti-ship missile is the Penguin (AGM-119B). It is a high subsonic, fire-and-forget missile that is launched from the underside of an SH-60B LAMPS III helicopter, found aboard *Spruance* destroyers, as well as on some of the most recently built *Arleigh Burke* destroyers. Originally designed for the Norwegian Navy, the Penguin entered U.S. service in 1993. It has a range of about 20 miles, an inertial guidance system, and infrared terminal homing. Launched from altitudes higher than 100 feet, the Penguin carries a 265-pound semi-armor piercing, high-explosive warhead on an indirect flight path from the helicopter to the hostile ship. The missile's electronics discriminate between targets and decoys along the way.

One of eight Tomahawk land-attack cruise missiles launches from the stern VLS of the USS *Laboon* (DDG-58) to attack selected air-defense targets in Iran on September 3, 1996, during Operation Desert Strike. The missile was launched at 7:15 AM local time in the North Arabian Gulf. It followed Saddam Hussein's offensive action into Kurdish territory. The Navy is now developing the next generation cruise missile, the Tactical Tomahawk, that will have a range of 1,600 nautical miles and be able to loiter over its target area for re-attack. *U.S. Navy*

As for sinking enemy submarines, the VLA aside, *Spruance* and *Arleigh Burke* destroyers are armed with the Mk-46 Lightweight torpedo, which is fired from two triple launchers. The Mk-46 Lightweight torpedo—NATO's standard for antisubmarine warfare—is a deep-diving, high-speed torpedo equipped with active/passive acoustic homing. After it hits the water, the torpedo begins a helical search pattern until it detects the enemy submarine. It then attacks at a speed of about 45 knots. If it misses, it automatically re-acquires the sub and continues with the attack. The torpedo has a range of about 7 miles and can dive to more than 1,200 feet. Its warhead consists of 95 pounds of high explosive.

Several *Spruance* and *Arleigh Burke* destroyers have received alterations in recent years that allow them to carry the Navy's newest torpedo, the Mk-50 Advanced Lightweight Torpedo, "Barracuda". It is similar to the Mk-46, but is faster, has greater endurance, and can dive deeper. It also has better terminal homing, a programmable digital computer, and more power to destroy. The 750-pound Barracuda is powered by a chemical-energy propulsion system that provides full power at all depths and can furnish multi-speed settings as required by the situation at hand. The Mk-50 reportedly has a speed in excess of 50 knots and a maximum diving depth of about 1,950 feet. Its warhead comprises a 100-pound high-explosive

A rigid-hull inflatable boat (RHIB) carrying a boarding team from the USS *Spruance* (DD-963) (background) heads to inspect a nearby merchant ship's cargo. Inspections and policing actions such as this are becoming fairly routine for the Navy in a post-Cold War environment. In this instance, the Navy is enforcing a United Nations embargo decree that states all commercial and private vessels entering Haiti are to be inspected for contraband. *U.S. Navy*

shaped charge. For maximum damage, the directed energy must penetrate the enemy sub's hull and not glance off.

Defense! Defense!

To protect themselves from aerial and surface attacks while under way at sea, destroyers rely on what is known as "point defense" weapons. These include the 5-inch Mk-45 gun, NATO Sea Sparrow, Rolling Airframe Missile, and the Phalanx Close-In Weapon System.

The 5-inch/54-caliber Mk-45 gun is capable of automatically firing up to 20 rounds per minute to a distance of nearly 14 miles against land targets and hostile ships, and 9 miles against enemy aircraft. The projectile, weighing in at 70 pounds, has a semi-active laser-guidance system. *Spruance* destroyers are armed with two 5-inch guns, mounted at the bow and stern, while *Arleigh Burke* destroyers have only one bow-mounted gun. Both destroyer classes deploy with 600 rounds of

Above: A close look at the NATO Sea Sparrow launcher mounted astern on the USS *Oldendorf* (DD-972). The missile itself is suspended from a railing inside the canister. The launcher, which has doors in the front and blow-out panels in the rear, can rotate not only left and right, but also up and down to line the missile up with the target. Unfortunately, the eight-cell launcher has to be reloaded by hand. Destroyers equipped with the Sea Sparrow deploy with 24 missiles. *S. F. Tomajczyk*

Left: When a destroyer's 5-inch gun fires a projectile, the casing is automatically ejected from the breech and lands on the ship's deck several feet away. Often, as this photograph shows, the edge of the casing slices into the nonskid surface, creating what sailors call a "smiley." The salt spray gets into the cut and causes the metal to rust, making the smile stand out. To prevent the deck from rusting away, sailors routinely replace the nonskid surface. *S. F. Tomajczyk*

From a distance, an *Arleigh Burke* destroyer, such as the USS *Stethem* (DDG-63) shown here, looks deceptively tame, but a practiced eye can detect several features. On the stern you'll note two round holes. They're for the two torpedo decoys ("Nixies") the ship streams behind it when at sea. There's another hole centered on the stern (not seen in this photo) for the ship's SQR-19 tactical towed sonar array. Moving forward is the flight deck for the LAMPS III ASW helicopter, followed by a 61-cell VLS and Mk-32 torpedo launchers. The crisscrossed tubes are eight Harpoon anti-ship missiles. The white domed item directly above the Harpoon is one of the ship's two CIWS. (The other is mounted forward of the bridge.) On the forward superstructure is one of the four SPY-1D "faces," which is tied in with the AEGIS combat system. On the bow is a 5-inch gun with 600 rounds of ammunition. Just behind it, and out of view in this photo, is a 29-cell VLS. *S. F. Tomajczyk*

ammunition in their magazines for each 5-inch gun they carry.

The NATO Sea Sparrow is an offspring of the Sparrow radar-guided air-to-air missile used by jet fighters. It is fired from an eight-tube Mk-29 launcher that is generally located toward the stern of a surface combatant that does not have Standard missile capabilities. The solid-propellant missile travels at a scorching 2,660 miles per hour and has a range of about 9 miles. The Sea Sparrow uses semi-active radar to home in on the hostile missile, and then destroys it with a blast-fragmentation warhead. *Spruance* destroyers have one Sea Sparrow launcher mounted aft of the helicopter deck that deploys to sea with 24 missiles. The *Arleigh Burke* destroyers do not carry Sea Sparrow launchers. Instead, they are armed with SM-2 (MR) missiles.

The deck may look cluttered, but space is at a premium aboard a destroyer, including the USS *Oldendorf* (DD-972) shown here. The round canisters in the upper left hold four Harpoon anti-ship missiles. No, they do not launch downward at the ocean's surface, they are angled to fire in the opposite direction. Their fiery plume, however, does blast at the water. Another four canisters are positioned on the other side of the destroyer and are angled to fire in this direction. In the upper right is a CIWS with its barrel covered. And directly below it is the SLQ-32, a radar-warning system that alerts the ship to incoming missiles using radar to home in on the destroyer. *S. F. Tomajczyk*

Since 1991, the Navy has been replacing its original Sea Sparrow system with the U.S./German-designed Rolling Airframe Missile (RAM), an advanced short-range fire-and-forget missile used against air threats. The missile, which rolls in flight to create an accurate three-dimensional targeting "picture," is 9 feet, 2 inches long; it has a 5-inch diameter and weighs 160 pounds. It uses existing technologies in its makeup: the infrared seeker from the Stinger

missile; and the solid-propellant rocket motor, fuse, and warhead from the Sidewinder missile. RAM has a range of about 5 miles, and can be fired from both Sea Sparrow launchers and its own uniquely designed 21-cell launcher. The missiles travel at Mach 2 speed. Several, but not all, *Spruance* destroyers carry a single RAM launcher that is mounted on the stern.

The Phalanx Close-In Weapon System (CIWS, pronounced "see whiz") is a 20mm

An ensign receives her second anthrax vaccination while deployed on the USS *Nicholson* (DD-982) during Operation Desert Fox. The risk of an enemy or terrorist group using chemical or biological warfare agents today against American military forces is increasing due to the fact that they are so easy to make and disperse. On the day before this photo was taken, December 18, 1998, the *Nicholson* had launched Tomahawk missiles at Iraq to reduce the nation's biological weapons manufacturing capabilities. *U.S. Navy*

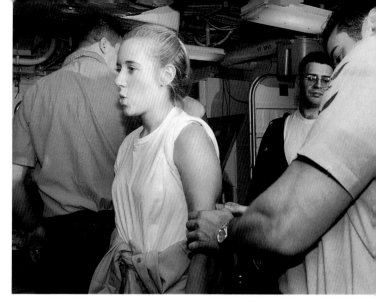

The USS *Paul F. Foster* (DD-964) (left) plows through moderate seas while refueling from the replenishment oiler USS *Wichita* (AOR-1) off the coast of San Diego. The time chosen for a warship to refuel depends on the operational fleet commander's assessment of what his ships need to maintain. In the Pacific Fleet, for instance, if a ship anticipates dropping below 60 percent of capacity before it can refuel, it has to notify the fleet commander. Also, when a ship ties up, it should be 90 percent full. The destroyers use JP5 and DFM (Diesel Fuel, Marine) for fuel. As it is used up, it is automatically replaced by sea water, which floats atop the fuel. This means the ship never gets lighter as it burns fuel. In prior years, a ship's loss of weight caused by burning fuel and not replacing it wreaked havoc on the ship's seaworthiness, especially in rough seas. *U.S. Navy*

Gatling-style gun with six barrels that fires 4,500 rounds per minute. With a range of less than a mile, it is a destroyer's *in extremis* weapon to protect itself from incoming aircraft and anti-ship missiles. The CIWS, which has a magazine capacity of 1,550 rounds, essentially creates a wall of armor-piercing, tungsten penetrators the missile has to fly through to reach the ship. The system uses radar to track the inbound missile, and a computer to determine where the gun must be pointed to strike the missile. The radar tracks both the missiles and the penetrators, and corrects the gun's aim to bring the two together. If two or more missiles are approaching, CIWS automatically analyzes the threat of each missile and reacts to the most dangerous threat first.

Unfortunately, with advancements in foreign anti-ship missile technology, the Navy has decided to replace the Phalanx CIWS with the RAM. The RAM is able to kill inbound cruise missiles at greater (and safer) distances from a destroyer. Yet, if you ask sailors, their preference is for the CIWS. They would much rather have a dense "cloud of lead" between them and an incoming cruise missile than a single RAM missile. Both destroyer classes are currently armed with CIWS. This replacement is already under way.

Sailors aboard the USS *O'Bannon* (DD-987) examine a RIM-7 Sea Sparrow surface-to-air missile before it is loaded into the launcher. *U.S. Navy*

Opposite: An HH-46A Sea Knight helicopter unloads supplies on the deck of the destroyer USS *O'Brien* (DD-975) during a vertical replenishment (VERTREP) operation. Destroyers need to be replenished with perishable food items about every two weeks, although they deploy with a 90-day supply of nonperishable items such as macaroni and canned goods. The Sea Knight is usually assigned to a supply ship. *U.S. Navy*

CHAPTER FIVE

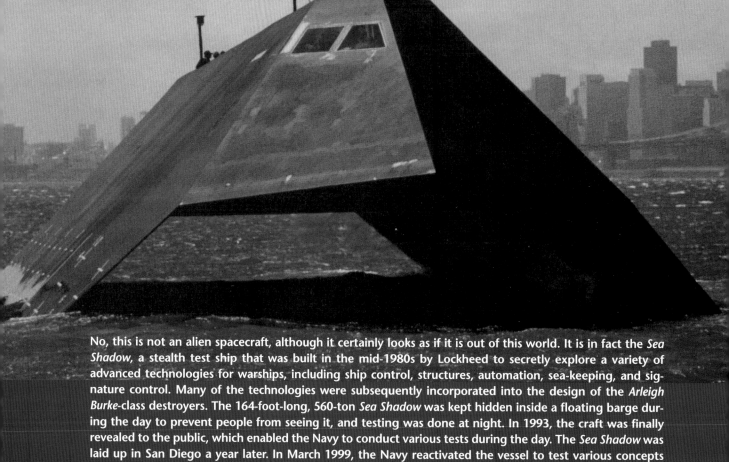

No, this is not an alien spacecraft, although it certainly looks as if it is out of this world. It is in fact the *Sea Shadow*, a stealth test ship that was built in the mid-1980s by Lockheed to secretly explore a variety of advanced technologies for warships, including ship control, structures, automation, sea-keeping, and signature control. Many of the technologies were subsequently incorporated into the design of the *Arleigh Burke*-class destroyers. The 164-foot-long, 560-ton *Sea Shadow* was kept hidden inside a floating barge during the day to prevent people from seeing it, and testing was done at night. In 1993, the craft was finally revealed to the public, which enabled the Navy to conduct various tests during the day. The *Sea Shadow* was laid up in San Diego a year later. In March 1999, the Navy reactivated the vessel to test various concepts and technologies that are slated to be incorporated into the *Zumwalt*-class DD-21 destroyer. *U.S. Navy*

A LOOK TO THE FUTURE
Surface Warfare Evolves Again

Since the dissolution of the Soviet Union in the early 1990s, the U.S. Navy has undergone a tremendous change. Instead of preparing for a nuclear war against an enormous Soviet fleet in the open oceans of the world, the Navy now finds itself responding to low-intensity conflicts and police actions in shallow, coastal waters around the globe where hostile forces may resort to using theater missiles and weapons of mass destruction. This includes searching merchant ships in the Persian Gulf for military contraband, enforcing the "No Fly" zone over Iraq, evacuating American citizens from dangerous situations abroad, and providing humanitarian aid to nations that have endured a natural disaster, such as the severe earthquake that struck Turkey in 1999.

An Extended Range Guided Munition (ERGM) test round for the DD-21 Land Attack Destroyer is fired at the Armys Yuma Proving Ground in Arizona. *Raytheon Company*

To comply with Quadrennial Defense Review mandates, the Navy has decommissioned, sold to foreign navies, or scrapped more than 200 ships since the Cold War ended in 1991. The fleet is now projected to have a total of 305 ships by 2002, of which only 116 will be surface combatants. Ironically, while the number of ships available for missions has plummeted, the demand for the Navy's warfighting capabilities has markedly increased. According to a Congressional Research Service study, U.S. armed forces (including the Navy) were used 16 times under President Reagan, 14 times under President Bush, and so far, more than 25 times under President Clinton.

A recent study done by the Department of the Navy came to similar conclusions. The report points out that during the Cold War, the Navy and Marine Corps responded to some 190 crises, an average of about 4 per year. In comparison, between 1990 and 1997, the Navy and Marine Corps responded to 75 crises, or more than 10 per year. In other words, double the Cold War rate.

With U.S. naval forces becoming increasingly involved in larger missions around the world, there is a growing realization in the Pentagon and on Capitol Hill that the fleet should be increasing in size instead of slimming down. Otherwise, the Navy will not have enough ships to respond to future crises.

As a result, the Navy's top commanders are now urging the service to buy back some 20 warships now scheduled to be decommissioned, including several *Spruance*-class destroyers. They also want to beef up the fleet of *Arleigh Burke*-class destroyers by acquiring five more through 2008 at $1 billion a piece. The current Pentagon budget mandates *Arleigh Burke*-class constructions to end in 2005.

A New Underwater Threat

Downsizing and high deployment tempo aside, the Navy is faced with still yet another predicament: enemy diesel submarines in the fleet. Once sneered at by military experts as being a low-tech, antiquated weapon platform that had severe war-fighting limitations, the diesel submarine now poses a threat to U.S. naval forces. The Navy finds itself routinely operating in shallow, claustrophobic waters around the world, such as the Persian Gulf. These areas are ideal for the small, elusive, and ultra-quiet diesel subs that run off batteries while submerged. Their skippers know the coastlines and underwater topography better than the United States because they operate in these waters all the time, thereby giving them a slight edge in combat.

"It's definitely a chess game," says Commander Roger Coldiron, commanding officer of the USS *Stump* (DD-978). "A diesel sub underwater is very quiet and difficult to detect, especially if he's below the (thermal) layer. It's a scary situation, but it's manageable.

"You have to remember he can't see underwater any better than I can. I know for sure, though, he's going to come up and take a look (through his periscope) before he shoots. Every time. When he does, there's a good chance I'll see his periscope on the screen."

Coldiron also points out that since a diesel submarine operates off batteries, sooner or later it has to surface to recharge them. "When he lights off his engines, we've got him."

But as advocates of Murphy's Law point out, there are no guarantees in combat. Given the right circumstances, a skilled diesel sub captain could indeed attack and sink a U.S. warship. That is why the Pentagon is so concerned about diesel subs, especially since dozens are estimated to be in operation around the world. Fortunately, both the *Spruance*- and *Arleigh Burke*-class destroyers are equipped with tremendous ASW sonar systems. While their passive sonars may have a difficult time detecting the presence of a silent-running diesel submarine, their active sonars—depending on the sea conditions at the time—generally do not.

New Technologies

To counter emerging combat threats such as the diesel submarine, the Navy continues to pursue aggressive research programs. Many of these high-tech projects involve the Navy's AEGIS combat system and destroyers. In addition to the Tactical Tomahawk missile, two of the more notable projects under way are the Navy Area Ballistic Missile Defense program and the Cooperative Engagement Capability program.

Ballistic Missile Defense

In 1998, the Rumsfeld Commission released a report stating that U.S. military forces were unequipped to defend against ballistic missiles. It also noted that in addition to North Korea and Iran, other rogue nations including Libya were developing such missiles, and that it was only a matter of time before the missiles would be used against the United States and its allies. In response, the Navy has aggressively pursued the Area Theater Ballistic Missile Defense program. AEGIS-equipped destroyers and cruisers will be outfitted with a

modified AEGIS combat system that will be able to detect and track short- to medium-range ballistic missiles, and shoot them down with a modified Standard missile (SM-2 Block IVA). This system, scheduled to be deployed aboard warships beginning in 2003, will enable the Navy to protect military forces at sea and ashore from enemy ballistic missiles.

A more advanced system, known as the Navy Theater Wide (NTW) ballistic missile defense program, will also use the AEGIS destroyers and cruisers to shoot down ballistic missiles. Only this time, they will do so against long-range missiles that are flying above the Earth's atmosphere. The system will use a new SM-3 version of the Standard missile outfitted with a special projectile that destroys a missile by ramming into it at high speeds. NTW is designed to defend the continental United States against the threat posed by the North Korean No-Dong, the Iranian Shihab-3, and similar long-range enemy ballistic missiles. If NTW is fully funded, the Navy says it can deploy a limited NTW system in the 2003 to 2004 time frame.

Cooperative Engagement Capability

To improve the lethality of its aircraft carrier battle groups, the Navy is merging AEGIS into a wireless network of sensor systems known as Cooperative Engagement Capability (CEC). CEC will allow warships to pass tactical information from one ship to another in real time, much like the way a football quarterback throws the football to a receiver. As with all tactical data, CEC/AEGIS information will be processed and put on display in a destroyer's combat information center.

When AEGIS is finally integrated into this network, it will enhance the fighting and survival capability of individual ships. Suppose, for instance, a destroyer detects an anti-ship missile flying from shore toward another destroyer positioned miles away on the horizon. Today, all the destroyer can do is alert the other warship by radio and pray that it is able

It may be the end of a long day aboard the USS *Fitzgerald* (DDG-62), but it is not the end of the mighty destroyer. For more than 130 years, the destroyer has successfully evolved—from torpedo boat to multi-mission destroyer—to meet the challenges of surface warfare and the introduction of new weapon systems. With the U.S. Navy being increasingly called upon to participate in police actions and low-intensity conflicts around the world, the destroyer will remain at the heart of the action, where it rightly belongs. *S. F. Tomajczyk*

to quickly detect the missile with its own sensors and shoot it down. With CEC/AEGIS, however, the destroyer can continue to track the missile and relay the data to the threatened destroyer, which then fires a salvo of SM-2 missiles at the hostile anti-ship missile using the forwarded information.

DD-21: The Once and Future Warrior

While the aforementioned projects are impressive, they pale in comparison with the capabilities of the Navy's next generation of 32 guided-missile destroyers, the *Zumwalt* class (DD-21). This class is named in honor of Admiral Elmo R. Zumwalt, Jr., the youngest man ever to serve as the Chief of Naval Operations and the man best known for revitalizing the Navy in the 1970s. The *Zumwalt* destroyers are unlike any that have set sail on the high seas before them. Currently being designed by two separate teams, the *Zumwalt* class is anticipated to have a radical outward appearance due to the stealthy features stipulated by the Navy, plus a slew of high-tech weapon systems.

Guns will be a major component of the DD-21, with the Navy deciding on a single-barrel, 155mm Advanced Gun System (AGS). The AGS will be capable of striking targets with great accuracy at a 100-mile range—far greater than today's 15-mile range. The 155mm shells will be able to penetrate armor and destroy tanks, thereby providing inland combat troops with tremendous gun-fire support. The AGS will fire 12 rounds per minute and will have a 600- to 750-round magazine capacity.

Another unique shell being designed for the 155mm gun is the Extended Range Guided Munition (ERGM) rocket shell. It is a weapon that will enable the Navy to provide deep fire support of Marine Corps forces as they quickly move ashore and inland during an amphibious assault. Essentially a small missile masquerading as a munition, the ERGM will use GPS satellites to fly to the intended area up to 63 nautical miles away. By comparison, today's shells have a maximum range of only 13 nautical miles. When the ERGM reaches the target, it will release a canister of 72 anti-personnel or anti-materiel submunitions at an altitude of 750 to 1,200 feet above the ground. These golf-ball-sized bomblets will wreak havoc when they explode, either killing enemy soldiers or destroying vehicles, buildings, and supply depots. A prototype of the ERGM—albeit a smaller version weighing in at only 100 pounds—is intended to be deployed on several *Arleigh Burke*-class destroyers and tested. In July 2000, the precommissioned *Churchill* (DDG-81) successfully test-fired the brand-new Mk-45 (Mod 4) 5-inch, 62-caliber naval gun that will be used to fire the ERGM in the future. The *Churchill* fired a total of 132 rounds during the test, which took place off the northeastern Georges Bank near Maine.

Supplementing the AGS, which is already being lauded as the "King of the Battlefield," will be the DD-21's several hundred missiles, including the Tactical Tomahawk and the still-evolving Advanced Land Attack Missile (ALAM).

Unlike any surface warship before it, the DD-21 will be outfitted with an electrical propulsion system instead of the more traditional gas-turbine engines. This revolutionary drive brings with it a host of advantages, namely quieter propulsion, more space for berthing, reduced maintenance, and fewer sailors to keep the system running. With regard to the crew number, designers intend for the DD-21 to be manned by just 95 persons. By comparison, today's *Arleigh Burke* destroyers carry a crew in excess of 300.

The Navy envisions buying 32 *Zumwalt*-class destroyers at a total cost of up to $25 billion, although senior commanders are now urging the service to purchase an additional 16 to enable the Navy to adequately respond to future crises.

When the USS *Zumwalt* finally joins the U.S. fleet around 2008, it will carry on the 130-year tradition of its predecessors. Armed to the teeth with high-tech weapon systems and possessing a cloak of stealth to prevent its detection by enemy forces, the DD-21 will stalk the high seas keeping evil at bay. It is through the threat of possibly using the DD-21's weapons that peace will be maintained.

Crew members of the USS *Hayler* (DD-997) man the rails as the destroyer passes the Statue of Liberty upon arriving in New York City. The *Hayler* is the 31st and last destroyer of the *Spruance* class. She originally was to have been a test bed to explore whether or not the *Spruance* design could handle four helicopters (instead of two) and V/STOL aircraft like the AV-8B Harrier and V-22 Osprey. In the end, however, the Navy decided it really needed another destroyer instead, and so the *Hayler* was built as a standard *Spruance*-class destroyer. The *Hayler* is scheduled to be decommissioned in 2013, marking the end of a remarkable class of multi-mission destroyers that kept the world free for nearly 40 years. *U.S. Navy*

APPENDICES
GLOSSARY

Air Slug – When high pressure air is used to test-fire a destroyer's torpedo launch system without actually launching a torpedo. Air slugs can be fired while the ship is at pierside.

ASROC – Antisubmarine rocket. See VLA

Blue Out – Slang for the failure of electronics, radars, and sonars on surface ships as a direct result of electromagnetic pulse (EMP). EMP is an intense but short-lived electric and magnetic field created by a nuclear explosion.

Brown Water – Nickname for the shallow, littoral regions of the world such as the Persian Gulf. The Navy is increasingly finding itself operating in these areas as opposed to deep, "blue water" oceans.

Cell – Nickname for the individual launch tubes that constitute the Vertical Launch System.

CG – Cruiser.

CIC – The combat information center, "the heart of a warship," is the central location where all tactical information is analyzed and displayed. On some ships, the CIC is known as the Combat Display Center or Combat Direction Center (CDC).

Commissioning Date – The date on which a ship officially enters service with the U.S. Navy and joins the fleet. At this time, the ship also receives its "USS" designation.

Davy Jones' Locker – In folklore, the bottom of the ocean where dead sailors reside.

DD – Destroyer.

DDG – Guided-missile destroyer.

Decommissioning Date – The date a ship's command is terminated.

DESRON – Destroyer Squadron, the basic organizational structure of surface warfare. A destroyer squadron generally comprises several destroyers and frigates, and is overseen by a captain. In an aircraft carrier battle group, the DESRON commander is referred to as "Commodore."

EMCOM – Emissions Control, the ability to control a ship's electromagnetic emissions. The greater the EMCOM, the less visible a ship becomes to enemy sensors.

Face – Nickname for the octagonal-shaped SPY-1 radar antenna.

FFG – Frigate.

Go Fast – In anti-surface warfare, jargon for a vessel moving faster than 20 knots.

Knee Knocker – The nickname for the steel thresholds you step over when walking down a passageway on surface ships. If you don't step high enough to clear it, you'll bang your shins.

Launch Date – The date a ship is released from the dry dock and slides into the water.

Noodle (Tail) – Nickname for the long sonar array towed behind a warship or submarine. The array is composed of sensitive hydrophones, which can detect enemy submarines by the noise they make.

Quadrennial Defense Review – A review done every four years to check military requirements.

Radar Cross Section (RCS) – The amount of radiation reflected off an object (missile, ship, aircraft) when struck by a radar beam. RCS is determined by several factors, including the curvature of the object's surface, the radar absorbency of the material being struck (foam absorbs radar better than metal), and the distance from the target to the emitting radar (the farther the distance, the weaker the return echo).

Redcrown – Code name for the ship in an aircraft carrier battle group (CVBG) that is responsible for coordinating the group's air defense efforts. The Redcrown ship is often a cruiser, although *Arleigh Burke*-class destroyers are also used, and it is usually positioned closest to the aircraft carrier.

Ring of Steel – Slang for the warships encircling an aircraft carrier at sea. Destroyers usually are located farthest away to defend against enemy submarines.

Rooster Tail – A distinctive tail-like wake produced by a fast-moving ship. The *Arleigh Burke*-class destroyers are well known for the rooster tails they kick up when traveling at speeds in excess of 32 knots.

Shaped charge – A directed, concentrated cone of explosive gas/plasma able to melt through steel. The direction of the charge is determined by how the explosive itself is molded.

SLCM – Submarine-launched cruise missile. Pronounced "slickum."

Slick – Slang for any SLQ-designated electronic countermeasure system. Examples include the SLQ-32 (a radar-warning system) and the SLQ-25 (a torpedo decoy that is towed behind ships to lure away incoming torpedoes).

Small Boy – Nickname for any warship smaller than an aircraft carrier. Specifically used in reference to a destroyer, cruiser, or frigate.

SSBN – Nuclear-powered, fleet ballistic missile.

SSN – Nuclear-powered attack submarine.

Stricken – Moved from active duty status determined by six conditions: lost or missing; damaged beyond economical repair; salvaged for essential equipment or parts; disposed of outside the United States pursuant to the policies of the Integrated Aeronautic Program; disposed of outside the United States as directed by the Commanding Naval Officer; or transferred from Navy custody.

THAWK – Nickname for a Tomahawk cruise missile. It is pronounced "tea hawk."

Tin Can – Nickname for a destroyer. The term was used during World War II in reference to a destroyer's thin hull plating—measuring a scant .125 inches thick—that was easily penetrated by machine-gun fire. Such ships offered sailors little more protection than a tin can.

UNREP – Underway replenishment, the resupplying and refueling of ships at sea. The replenishment ship pulls alongside the target ship and, using strung cables, sends across provisions and fuel lines.

VERTREP – Vertical replenishment, the resupplying of ships at sea using helicopters. The provisions are slung beneath the helicopter in a special cargo net.

VLA – Vertical Launch ASROC. An antisubmarine missile that is fired from a destroyer's Mk-41 VLS. The VLA is a short-range missile that uses the Mk-46 acoustic-homing torpedo as its warhead.

VLS – Vertical Launch System. A missile-launching system in which a missile (Tomahawk, Standard, VLA) is stored and fired from a vertical position in a sealed launch tube. Destroyers use the Mk-41 VLS, which is embedded into the ship's hull. VLS are designed to carry either 29 or 61 missiles.

DESTROYER DATA

Name	Hull No.	Launched	Homeport
Arleigh Burke Class			
USS Arleigh Burke*	DDG-51	1989	Norfolk, VA
USS Barry	DDG-52	1991	Norfolk, VA
USS John Paul Jones*	DDG-53	1991	San Diego, CA
USS Curtis Wilbur*	DDG-54	1992	Yokosuka, Japan
USS Stout	DDG-55	1992	Norfolk, VA
USS John S. McCain*	DDG-56	1992	Yokosuka, Japan
USS Mitscher	DDG-57	1993	Norfolk, VA
USS Laboon*	DDG-58	1993	Norfolk, VA
USS Russell	DDG-59	1993	Pearl Harbor, HI
USS Paul Hamilton*	DDG-60	1993	Pearl Harbor, HI
USS Ramage	DDG-61	1994	Norfolk, VA
USS Fitzgerald*	DDG-62	1994	San Diego, CA
USS Stethem	DDG-63	1994	San Diego, CA
USS Carney*	DDG-64	1994	Mayport, FL
USS Benfold	DDG-65	1994	San Diego, CA
USS Gonzalez*	DDG-66	1995	Norfolk, VA
USS Cole	DDG-67	1995	Norfolk, VA
USS The Sullivans*	DDG-68	1995	Mayport, FL
USS Milius	DDG-69	1995	San Diego, CA
USS Hopper*	DDG-70	1996	Pearl Harbor, HI
USS Ross	DDG-71	1996	Norfolk, VA
USS Mahan*	DDG-72	1996	Norfolk, VA
USS Decatur*	DDG-73	1996	San Diego, CA
USS McFaul	DDG-74	1997	Norfolk, VA
USS Donald Cook*	DDG-75	1997	Norfolk, VA
USS Higgins*	DDG-76	1997	San Diego, CA
USS O'Kane*	DDG-77	1998	Pearl Harbor, HI
USS Porter	DDG-78	1997	Norfolk, VA
Oscar Austin*	DDG-79	1998	Not yet announced
Roosevelt	DDG-80	1999	Not yet announced
Winston S. Churchill*	DDG-81	1999	Not yet announced
Lassen	DDG-82	1999	Not yet announced
Howard*	DDG-83	1999	Not yet announced
Bulkeley	DDG-84	Under construction	
McCampbell*	DDG-85	Under construction	
Shoup	DDG-86	Under construction	
Mason*	DDG-87	Under construction	
Preble	DDG-88	Under construction	
Mustin	DDG-89	Under construction	
Chafee*	DDG-90	Under construction	
Pinckney	DDG-91	Under construction	
TBA*	DDG-92	Under contract	
TBA	DDG-93	Under contract	
TBA*	DDG-94	Under contract	
TBA	DDG-95	Under contract	
TBA*	DDG-96	Under contract	
TBA	DDG-97	Under contract	
TBA	DDG-98	Under contract	
TBA*	DDG-99	Under contract	
TBA	DDG-100	Under contract	
TBA*	DDG-101	Under contract	

Name	Hull No.	Launched	Homeport
Spruance Class			
USS *Spruance*	DD-963	1975	Mayport, FL
USS *Paul F. Foster*	DD-964	1976	Everett, WA
USS *Kinkaid*	DD-965	1976	San Diego, CA
USS *Hewitt*	DD-966	1976	San Diego, CA
USS *Elliot*	DD-967	1976	San Diego, CA
USS *Radford*	DD-968	1977	Norfolk, VA
USS *Peterson*	DD-969	1977	Norfolk, VA
USS *Caron*	DD-970	1977	Norfolk, VA
USS *David R. Ray*	DD-971	1977	Everett, WA
USS *Oldendorf*	DD-972	1978	San Diego, CA
USS *John Young*	DD-973	1978	San Diego, CA
USS *Comte de Grasse*	DD-974	1978	Decommissioned
USS *O'Brien*	DD-975	1977	Yokosuka, Japan
USS *Merrill*	DD-976	1978	Decommissioned
USS *Briscoe*	DD-977	1978	Norfolk, VA
USS *Stump*	DD-978	1978	Norfolk, VA
USS *Conolly*	DD-979	1978	Decommissioned
USS *Moosebrugger*	DD-980	1978	Mayport, FL
USS *John Hancock*	DD-981	1979	Mayport, FL
USS *Nicholson*	DD-982	1979	Norfolk, VA
USS *John Rodgers*	DD-983	1979	Decommissioned
USS *Leftwich*	DD-984	1979	Decommissioned
USS *Cushing*	DD-985	1979	Yokosuka, Japan
USS *Harry W. Hill*	DD-986	1979	Decommissioned
USS *O'Bannon*	DD-987	1979	Mayport, FL
USS *Thorn*	DD-988	1980	Norfolk, VA
USS *Deyo*	DD-989	1980	Norfolk, VA
USS *Ingersoll*	DD-990	1980	Decommissioned
USS *Fife*	DD-991	1980	Everett, WA
USS *Fletcher*	DD-992	1980	Pearl Harbor, HI
USS *Kidd*	DD-993	1981	Decommissioned
USS *Callaghan*	DD-994	1981	Decommissioned
USS *Scott*	DD-995	1981	Decommissioned
USS *Chandler*	DD-996	1982	Decommissioned
USS *Hayler*	DD-997	1983	Norfolk, VA

Source: *Naval Vessel Registry*

*Ships marked with an asterisk were built by Bath Iron Works, all others built by Ingalls Shipbuilding.

Note: The date a ship is launched is not the same date it is commissioned. A warship is usually commissioned within a year or so after launching—sooner if the ship is needed for war. The time between launching and commissioning is reserved for the shipyard to finish outfitting the ship with electronics, weapon systems, insulation, and radars, as well as to complete the necessary painting of the hull and superstructures. This is followed by a series of sea trials, in which the ship is actually taken to sea and her various systems tested to ensure they work properly. If they don't, repairs and adjustments are made until everything works as it should. When the ship is finally commissioned, she enters service with the Navy and joins the fleet. This is the time when the ship receives the official "USS" designation before its name. The launch date is generally used to determine the age of a ship.

INDEX